WHAT'S NEXT?

Books by
H. Norman Wright

A Better Way to Think
The Complete Book of Christian Wedding Vows
*Finding Hope When Life Goes Wrong**
Healing for the Father Wound
Helping Those Who Hurt
*Loving Your Mother Without Losing Your Mind****
Making Peace With Your Past
*Making Peace With Your Mom****
Recovering from the Losses in Life
What's Next?

*With Matt Woodley and Julie Woodley
**With Sheryl Wright McCauley

WHAT'S NEXT?

NAVIGATING TRANSITIONS TO
MAKE THE REST *of* YOUR LIFE COUNT

H. NORMAN WRIGHT

BETHANY HOUSE PUBLISHERS

a division of Baker Publishing Group
Minneapolis, Minnesota

Published by Bethany House Publishers
11400 Hampshire Avenue South
Bloomington, Minnesota 55438
www.bethanyhouse.com

Bethany House Publishers is a division of
Baker Publishing Group, Grand Rapids, Michigan

Printed in the United States of America

Library of Congress Cataloging-in-Publication Data
Wright, H. Norman.
    What's next? : navigating transitions to make the rest of your life count / H. Norman Wright.
        p.   cm.
    Includes bibliographical references.
    Summary: "Experienced and trusted Christian counselor helps adults adapt to
and live with change and loss, discover the difference between aging and getting old,
and discover new purpose in the 'second half' of life"—Provided by publisher.
    ISBN 978-0-7642-0963-5 (pbk. : alk. paper)
    1. Life change events. 2. Change (Psychology) 3. Aging—Psychological aspects.
    I. Title.
BF637.L53W76 2012
155.67'2—dc23   2011040753

12   13   14   15   16   17   18   8   7   6   5   4   3   2

green
press
INITIATIVE

Contents

Introduction

Three older adults—another couple and I—sat around a table at Starbucks, talking and laughing. While we've been friends for decades, through the years our getting together had become less frequent.

We spent some time catching up, then after a while I asked, "What would you say are your dreams and plans for the next twenty years?"

Silence.

Slowly, they looked at one another and then back at me, puzzled.

"Honestly, we don't think in those terms," she said. "I'm seventy; I've been retired two years. We're trying to figure out what to do with our home, how to handle Medicare, maybe we'll be raising a grandchild, and who knows what. We're looking month to month! And I don't think we *have* twenty years. It'd be nice, especially if we had money, health, and energy, but . . ."

"For a moment, though," I said, "just assume you *do* have that window of time. How would you want to live it? What would you do? What could you accomplish? Sure, we're all older, but who knows what's still ahead of us?"

"You know," he said, "recently someone suggested that one means by which we could learn to start thinking this way is if each of us went through every day asking, 'What's next, Lord?' "

Have you considered what God's plans are for you? What might He have in store for you? How can you make the most of what's before you?

I've often asked a series of questions like this—"Where do you think you're headed?" and "What do you want at this stage?" and "Have you given any thought to that?"—and often I hear answers like the following:

"I don't know." "I'm not sure." "Hmm . . . not really."

Then I may say, "How about creating a plan for your life's next season?"

"My what?"

Simple queries, nothing profound. The answers, or lack of, speak volumes about our present and future.

Yes, you're getting older. I am too. Even so, we have choices. Here's a crucial one: We can fight the process, or we can embrace it.

One thing I've learned is *not* to fight the inevitable. In the face of something you cannot change, accept it. Embrace it. Go with it. I've seen so many people resist getting older; usually they're afraid of what it means. But resistance doesn't work.

Here's another issue: It's easy to "just let life happen" as we move on into and then through our fifties, sixties, and seventies.

However, if there's any time in life not to let that happen, it's now. True, our life as we age will be different. There'll be more unknowns and surprises we can't control. We'll certainly be challenged, and undoubtedly we'll face some changes we don't want. Nevertheless, in different and perhaps surprising ways, we can contribute; we can thrive; we can vitally enjoy life.

I'm reminded of one older man who did just that. Part of Caleb's story is recorded in the book of Joshua.

> Caleb . . . said to [Joshua], "You know what the Lord said to Moses the man of God . . . about you and me. I was forty years old when Moses the servant of the Lord sent me . . . to explore the land. And I brought him back a report according to my convictions, but my brothers who went up with me made the hearts of the people melt with fear. I, however, followed the Lord my God *wholeheartedly.* So on that day Moses swore to me, 'The land on which your feet have walked will be your inheritance and that of your children forever, because you have followed the Lord my God *wholeheartedly.*'
>
> "Now then, just as the Lord promised, he has kept me alive for forty-five years since [then]. . . . So here I am today, eighty-five years old! I am still as strong today as the day Moses sent me out; I'm just as vigorous to go out to battle now as I was then. Now give me this hill country that the Lord promised me that day. You yourself heard then that the Anakites were there and their cities were large and fortified, but, the Lord helping me, I will drive them out just as he said."
>
> Then Joshua blessed Caleb . . . and gave him Hebron as his inheritance. So Hebron has belonged to Caleb . . . ever since, because he followed the Lord, the God of Israel, *wholeheartedly.*[1]

Wholeheartedly is a word we don't hear very often, or at least often enough. It's even rarer that we see its presence, though I've met some whose life could be described that way. Most of the time, in my experience, "*wholehearted* people" are relatively young.

But it's possible for you and for me. This is the attitude God wants us to have about life, about Him, and about what we do, whether we're twenty or ninety. *Wholehearted* means being devoted, determined, enthusiastic, free from reserve or hesitation.

I ask myself how I manifest this trait. And I would ask you the same.

Perhaps, as for Caleb, this element is what gives us the most out of life.

Caleb never held back. He did everything wholeheartedly.

He was a man of convictions, and he lived by them.

He loved a challenge.

He had faith that the God of his youth was the God of his older age.

He was not limited by fear, even when others were.

In light of his example, what kind of older person do you want to be?

You're about to embark on a journey, one I hope is enlightening and perhaps a bit sobering. It's the journey of the rest of your life. We'll talk about what it could be like, or what it already is, and where you might go from here.

In response to this book's title you may say, "Yes, what *is* next? I'd like to know—especially the good news." Or maybe you'll say, "I'm not sure I want to know. Getting older doesn't appeal to me much."

Think about it in this way: The more you know, the fewer surprises you may face and the better prepared you can be. There may be some chapters ahead that don't seem to apply to you, perhaps some you'd rather avoid. But if you're over fifty (or not quite fifty), I think you'll see yourself here. You'll interact with elements like aging, midlife, empty nest, boomerang kids, and being alone again. You might consider leading an even more reflective life and ponder the legacy you're leaving. (You *are* leaving one.)

My prayer is that this, a book of possibilities, certainties, and choices, can serve to give you hope and, if you need one, a new purpose.

A wholehearted one.

1

Transitions: Friend or Foe?

From birth until death, life contains (some would say *is*) a series of transitions. A transition, for our purposes here, is a bridge between two different stages of life—a period of movement between states of relative certainty. It's a season of uncertainty, of change, as one stage winds down and a new one emerges. As you know, any change—even change that's predictable and expected—carries elements of risk, insecurity, and vulnerability.

Life is not a progression of fixed points. In fact, stable times actually are the exception; transition is the norm. Dr. Charles Sell uses an apt analogy:

Transitions are mysterious, like an underground passageway I once saw in a tour of a castle. The castle's rooms were gigantic, the woodwork extravagant, and the huge beams in the inner part of the towers projected massive strength. But what captivated me the most was that underground escape route. . . .

The vast ballroom offered its visitors the feeling of dignity. A sense of comfort overtook us in the luxurious bedroom suites. Serenity filled the garden room. But the secret tunnel was mysterious and unnerving. It held no comfortable chairs because it was not a place to rest. No artwork adorned its moist, dark stone walls. It wasn't made for stopping—it was en route, with a sense of urgency toward either past [castle behind] or future [stables ahead].

Life's transitions are like that, going *from* somewhere *to* somewhere. The present circumstances may seem like a void. It would be pleasant to turn back to the security left behind. But because that is impossible, it is necessary to keep groping for what is ahead; then there will surely be a resting place. . . .

The future simultaneously beckons with a mixture of hope and fear. Sometimes depression opens its dark pit. Above, the grass is green, the sun shines on gleeful men, women and children. But those in transition feel distant . . . pressured by the urgency to get on, to get through and out. Each transition carries with it the death of the previous state and the birth of a new one.[1]

I recently posed two questions to several people: "What have been the main transitions and issues you've faced in each phase of life's second half?" and "How did you handle them in a constructive way?" One man replied:

Retirement and the gradual disappearance of my body are the two main issues at this time. Other issues have surfaced because of them, though, such as social connections; self-actualization; how I relate to myself; and preparation for my eventual departure from this life. The central question in all my issues is *who do I wish to be*, not what do I wish to do.

I suppose having prostate cancer, a heart attack, and kidney disease should probably be included here, but only the latter is a current concern. Ultimately, I think there's really only one issue: Am I accepting and compassionate toward myself? That determines how I relate to others and the rest of the world.

[As for handling the issues constructively,] there's a line in one of my favorite poems that says,

> What you can plan
> is too small
> for you to live.
>
> What you can live
> wholeheartedly
> will make plans
> enough for the vitality
> hidden in your sleep.[2]

For example, writing poetry was never part of my [conscious] plan for bringing vitality to my life, yet it happened anyway.

What's worked well for me is being attentive to my existence and the world around me and being willing to let go of *my* plans (yes, I still make plans) when life presents other plans *for* me. After my cancer surgery, recovering in the hospital, I had a transformational experience centered around an orderly, mopping the hallway after midnight. I saw with "new eyes" something ordinary. It was also an awakening of self-compassion. Now I attempt to go through life with my eyes wide open.

Transition: Certainty and Change

To some, the word *change* holds a sense of hope, connoting fresh possibilities or the potential for newness, and they embrace it accordingly. To others, even the word itself represents a threat, a disruption of comfort and safety, and they resist it as such. Some make outward or cosmetic changes but intentionally strive to keep the essence of everything statically the same.

Perhaps this is the most straightforward way to conceptualize the process of genuine transition: The old, or what has been, dies so that the new can be born. A transition *starts* with an ending: We release the old to make way for the new. One reason change seems difficult is that even if what we had was flawed and we've known it, we're familiar with it and it's comfortable.

A transition has three "parts": an ending, a neutral zone, and a beginning. Here's what William Bridges, in *The Way of Transition*, said about the phases:

- In the ending, we lose or let go of our old outlook, our old reality, our old attitudes, our old values, our old self-image. We may resist this ending for a while. We may try to talk ourselves out of what we are feeling, and when we do give in, we may be swept by feelings of sadness and anger. . . .

- Next, we find ourselves in the neutral zone between the old and new—yet not really being either the old or the new. This confusing state is a time when our lives feel as though they have broken apart or gone dead. We get mixed signals, some from our old way of being and some from a way of being that is still unclear to us. Nothing feels solid. Everything is up for grabs. Yet for that very reason, it is a time when we sometimes feel that anything is possible. So the in-between time can be a very creative time too.

- Finally, we take hold of and identify with some new outlook and some new reality, as well as new attitudes and a new self-image. When we have done this, we feel that we are finally starting a new chapter in our lives. No matter how impossible it was to imagine a future earlier, life now feels as though it is back on its track again. We have a new sense of ourselves, a new outlook, and a new sense of purpose and possibility.[3]

Many endings end up as losses (either actual or perceived). None of us cares for losses, but they, too, are a necessary part of life. Though *loss* is a constant companion, we don't frequently talk about it—as if there's a silent conspiracy, we seem to have an unspoken agreement with others to avoid it.

14

Somehow we must come to realize, though, that with every loss comes the potential for change, for growth, for insight, for understanding, and for refinement. All of these are positive descriptions; they're words of hope.

There's no way around it: Life is a blending of loss and gain, subtraction and acquisition. In creation, loss is the ingredient of growth. A bud isn't a bud anymore by the time it's turned into a beautiful rose. A plant that pushes its way up through the soil is no longer a seed.

When you were a child, your baby teeth came in after bouts of pain and tears. Then, over time, they began to loosen and wiggle, and eventually they fell out or were pulled. They were lost to make room for permanent teeth.

Maybe it will lessen our discomfort somewhat if we replace *losses* with the word *endings*. We all have a life history of those. Can you remember the endings you've experienced throughout the past decade? What about over the past thirty years? Which endings did you face as a child?

Some people deny endings; some delay them or try to minimize their significance. Some tend to believe that things simply will happen as they happen, no matter what. Some want to barge right through their endings and move on. (For instance, time and time again I've seen this after the loss of a spouse— many try to bypass grief and quickly establish a new life.[4])

Think about the endings you've experienced most recently. Briefly reflect on them and then describe the way or style in which you handled them.

Ending	Style

15

Looking at your list, what would you say is your primary style? Is it abrupt? Does denial play a part? Are you usually slow and deliberate? Are you active, seeking to be a determining factor in what takes place? Are you passive, allowing events to situate you like a leaf in the wind? Do you get directly involved? Do you draw others into the process?

What You See, What You Get

Often, when people talk about endings or losses, even if they're moving on, they're past-focused. That is, though they have a new future, their focus is on the ending itself. "I lost _____ six months ago . . . a year ago . . . three years ago" (etc.).

Do you find yourself doing this? What might happen in terms of your hope, your optimism, even your joy, if instead of (or in addition to) saying, "*That* ended . . ." you said, "*This* started"? That's not ignoring or denying the ending; it's conveying that you won't let it consume your life, that you won't permit it to keep you from heading forward. We can fixate on endings . . . or we can focus on beginnings. Accepting the ending of a phase *is* a beginning![5]

> When we resist transition, we resist one or more of the three phases of its makeup. We may resist *letting go* of the old; we may resist the confusion of the in-between *neutral zone* state; or we may resist the uncertainties of making a risky new *beginning*. We resist transition not because we can't accept the change, but because we can't accept letting go of that piece of ourselves that we have to give up when and because the situation has changed.[6]

In this book we'll be looking mainly at common second-half transitions. These include going from being single to being married, from the twenties to the thirties, from the thirties to the forties, from being a couple to being parents, from being parents to the empty nest, from the empty nest to becoming grandparents, from being employed to retirement, and more. The fairly predictable transitions can be planned for, to reduce adjustment.

But most people do not plan adequately and are unaware as the next stage approaches and then encroaches. Suddenly they feel carried away by a flood, fully out of control. There are unexpected events, also, that occur *amidst* predictable changes: miscarriage, loss of a job, separation and divorce, illness, disability, death of a loved one, relocation of household, parents moving in, an adolescent running away or using drugs, an accident, a fire, a drop in socioeconomic status, natural disasters . . . it seems the list never ends.

Further, some of us take on additional new roles, like becoming a part-time student while continuing as a homemaker or full-time employee, or becoming a foster parent while still parenting our own children. We may even exchange one significant role for another—say, from full-time student to full-time employee. Whether it's a desired, anticipated transition or an unwelcomed, traumatic intrusion, the following expressions are among the feelings and perceptions you may experience in general during change:

exciting	scary
positive	necessary
stressful	uncomfortable
an attitude	awkward
a lot of work	essential for maturity
hard	refreshing
threatening	the opposite of death
a crossroads	like walking through a minefield
easier for some than others	an opportunity for self-examination
painful	easier to require in others
unavoidable	a tremendous source of fear

17

If you're a person who wants to keep your life the way it's been—if you usually or always resist transition—then think about this: How did you get to where you are in the first place? Part of the means of arriving at your present was change. Whether any given change was subtle or all-encompassing, and whether it seemed to consume you or you weren't even aware of it, change *happened*.

"Change" can mean to make different; to take a new course or direction; to replace one thing with another; to shift from one state to another; to undergo transformation; to introduce a substitution. In regard to most of these possibilities, though, many people consider change itself to be negative—they feel that change intrinsically represents or implies inferiority . . . instability . . . inadequacy . . . failure. No wonder, then, that they resist or even run from it.

Events You Might *Not* Expect

Let's look at the impact of abrupt, unpredictable changes. From this sample list,[7] please rank these potentially life-changing events in order of importance, or "upsetting potential," were they to occur in your life. What would you say would be the six most troubling events?

- Major illness in the family *(Karen, Matthew)*
- Jail sentence *(grandson)*
- Unfaithful spouse *Aon in law Mark*
- Being fired
- Miscarriage or stillbirth
- Divorce
- Unwanted pregnancy
- Court appearances *Karen*
- Death of a child

- Death of a spouse
- Major financial difficulty
- Business failure
- Marital separation due to argument
- Unemployment for a month
- Taking out a large loan
- Broken engagement
- Academic failure
- Child married without family approval
- Lawsuit
- Loss of personally valued objects
- Death of a close friend
- Demotion
- Major personal illness
- Start of an extramarital affair

Again, while many changes are at least somewhat predictable and can be planned for in advance so as to lessen their intensity, unpredictable changes that suddenly loom can shake us. A promised and needed promotion falls through. A spouse becomes gravely ill. A child is born with a severe defect. An adult son or daughter's relationship goes badly south.

Here's one man's experience facing unanticipated change:

Marrying at fifty-two; losing my wife to lung cancer at fifty-six; starting a new career at fifty-nine; remarrying at sixty; losing my business due to hostile takeover (along with all my investment and retirement) . . . at sixty-one; having my new wife desert and divorce me . . . after wiping out [our] balance of savings at sixty-two; and having to start everything all over again at age sixty-three . . . aside from all of this, life has been a piece of cake.

"How did you handle these changes in a constructive way?"

The only way I knew how to—turning to God and asking Him what there was that He was trying to show me, what He was trying to teach me, [what He was] training and preparing me for. Also, turning to friends for insights and help.

"What do you wish you'd done differently?"

With my wife who died, absolutely nothing, as it was the most loving experience of my life; we married quickly but knew this was where God wanted us to be. The loss of my business came totally out of left field—I didn't see it coming—but in hindsight I and my partners were too trusting and found out the hard way that there are bad people who, if they see a chance to take what's not theirs, will do what it takes. My marriage loss was the hardest of experiences to get over, as I trusted too much and didn't listen to friends or pay attention to red flags. . . . I didn't think a Christian woman would marry for any reason other than wanting to love and be loved at this stage of life, and I was terribly wrong.

Some of those events aren't common, and certainly their confluence isn't a regular norm. Even so, consider the relational impact of unforeseen change:

Any sudden change becomes a threat to whatever marital balance has been achieved. It tends to reawaken personal insecurities that the marriage has successfully overcome or held in check. You've noticed how sick people tend to fall back into childish ways—they become terribly dependent, demanding, unreasonable. Similarly, some people regress in other kinds of emotional crises. Long-conquered patterns of behavior reassert themselves at least until the first impact of the shock has been absorbed.[8]

Fortunately, we don't need satellite forecasts to tell us that certain transitions are coming, and they needn't become major storms in our lives. Consider your age and current stage: What's the next likely "main event" on your horizon? You can begin preparing for it by mentally rehearsing. For example, what will you do—to what things will you respond, and what things will you initiate? What will you rely on? In whom and in what will you invest? What new information will you gather to assist in the transition process? Which plans might you start making now, and at what points could you begin initiating them?

Taking Inventory, Making Plans

Sometimes we're moving along so quickly, so automatically, that we fail to recognize not only the changes but also the causes. Think for a moment about what's taken place in your life in the last year, or the last two years. Which events have brought about change?

For instance, what relationships have changed? Who has left, be it through death, or moving, or alienation, and whether it be family, friends, pets, colleagues, a public figure, a minister . . . ?

What has changed personally? Illness, success, failure, sleep difficulties, burnout, depression, weight gain or loss, appearance, lifestyle . . . ?

Any vocational or financial changes—getting fired or hired, changing jobs or responsibilities, decrease or increase in income, new loan or mortgage, having advancement blocked, promotion or demotion . . . ?

Changes in these and other areas can engender inner changes as well—they can impact political beliefs, spiritual convictions, self-esteem, perception of/respect for others, death or birth of dreams, one's sense of personal achievement or diminishment, and so on.[9]

In the face of transition, here's something we must learn how to begin doing up front: We need to identify the *focal point* of our particular difficulty with making the adjustment. Whether the issue is a normal life change or a sudden and unpredictable event, many obstacles people encounter during transition center on one of the following:

1. You could be having difficulty separating from the past stage. Maybe you're uncomfortable with your new role.

2. You could be having difficulty making a decision about what new path to take or plan of action to follow in order to negotiate the transition.

3. You could be having difficulty carrying out this decision for lack of understanding about what's involved in making the change. Perhaps you perceive that you lack enough knowledge or other resources that are needed to make the change secure.

4. You may already be in the midst of the transition but having difficulty weathering the period of adjustment until the change has stabilized. (Here, too, you could be lacking a resource that's needed to make the change secure.)

A teacher who realized he'd have to retire in ten years determined to expand his interests. He began to take local college courses in subjects he thought might interest him. He took up photography and began reading in areas he'd never before considered. He also began developing a list of projects he'd like to tackle, health and finances permitting, upon retirement.

Since there would be a significant loss in his life—his job and his livelihood—he planned in advance for a variety of replacements and worked through some feelings of loss. He also had the foresight to develop hobbies he could enjoy whether his health was good or poor. By anticipating, he eliminated the possibility of the transition becoming a crisis. That's important, because many men have a difficult and often unsuccessful adjustment when they retire. Depression is too common, and the male rate of suicide more than doubles after passing age sixty-five.

If moving through its stages were smooth and predictable, life would be fairly easy for most relatively mature individuals. *But,* first, many of us aren't yet sufficiently mature—we often don't take responsibility because we're stuck in our own development at an earlier stage. (To put it one way, we may have lived fifty or fifty-five years but emotionally still be "age thirty.") And second, again, some changes either land like sudden invaders or do not occur in the time sequence we'd anticipated.

Further, some roles aren't replaced by other duties after they expire. For instance, if you retire from work without finding a fulfilling task in retirement, or if you lose a spouse without remarrying, you experience a void. At the same time there can be physical changes like loss of hearing, confinement to a wheelchair, rapid or gradual gain or loss of weight.

Most people have heard the term "male midlife crisis," yet most men don't have such an experience; it isn't inevitable. All men do go through midlife transition, a normal change, but we can fairly accurately predict the candidate for a full-blown crisis. He's the person who

1. builds his sense of identity upon his work or occupation—that's his source of meaning;
2. is out of touch with his emotions and hasn't developed the ability to accept and express them;

3. hasn't learned to establish close, intimate friendships with other men.

This is a simplified evaluation, but it does hold true for many. A man needn't go through this crisis, which in most cases also creates crisis for his family and for others. He has a choice.

A crisis can emerge from an event not taking place "on time," such as with the "empty nest" stage of the family cycle. Many mothers face an adjustment when the last child leaves home. Though this predictable stage can be planned for in advance, it's when the child *doesn't* leave home at the intended time that a crisis often occurs, for parent, for child, or for both.[10]

My wife and I entered the empty nest approximately seven years ahead of schedule. When our daughter departed to be on her own, we should have been left with a thirteen-year-old son. But because he was severely disabled he'd left home at eleven for Salem Christian Home in Ontario, California.

We'd planned two years for his leaving. Praying, talking, making specific plans, and designing steps to follow meant his and our daughter's moves were fairly easy transitions. However, a year and a half later our daughter said she wanted to come home and live for a while, and this was a more difficult adjustment. We'd adjusted to the empty nest. We liked it. And we hadn't expected her to return.

Why is timing such an important factor? Think about it this way: What happens if your child doesn't reach high school on schedule? Or your certain promotion is delayed two years? Or your twenty-year-old doesn't move out and decides to live at home indefinitely? Or, when your spouse retires at sixty, you discover you have to work four more years?

For one thing, having an event happen "too early" or "too late"—according to our planning or foresight—can deprive us of the support of others who are the same or close to the same age. A woman wanting a child around twenty-eight who ends up not having one until thirty-seven may not enjoy the types of relationships she has desired with other women her age. At thirty-seven, many or most other mothers have children older than hers and aren't likely to be in the same stage or phase.

An off-schedule event may also deprive you of the sense of pride and satisfaction that often accompanies it. For example, if you refine your program for advancement, what happens if that long-sought promotion occurs a year before retirement, fifteen years after you hoped for or expected it? Is this recognition for accomplishment or merely a token gesture?

If an event occurs "too early," we may be limited in our plans and feel unprepared for our new roles. A mother widowed young must support her family during a time when most of her friends are couples. The oldest son must quit high school to help in the family business because of the unexpected crisis. And, if too many such events occur at once or close in proximity, we tend to fold when the last straw hits us.

Preparations for Transition

One man, facing the crisis of his wife being seriously ill in the hospital, then faced a major threat to his business the next day. Instead of attempting to juggle the handling of both, he determined that his wife's recovery was more important and that nothing would deter him from helping her. Because in his own mind the business crisis receded in importance, the scenario didn't drive up his stress level as we might expect. By deciding as he did, he was able to stay on top of the issues he prioritized.

Here are some suggestions for approaching or being in the midst of transition:

1. **Look at the life stage you're leaving.** Are you in any way fighting departure? Is there anything you don't want to relinquish or change? What's uncomfortable about the new role? What would help you find peace in embracing it? Find someone with whom you can discuss these issues.

2. If you're having difficulty making a decision regarding a new change or struggling to determine what plan to follow, seek the advice of someone you respect and whose insights will help you.

3. Make a list of what's involved in the changes at this stage. Do some research; do some reading; ask others about their own experience. *(asked Jean McQuay about loss of turn.)*

4. Identify specifically what you will need to do to obtain or hold on to some control in your situation. "Control" doesn't mean you have all the answers or know when or how the situation will resolve. Being "in control" means you've given yourself permission *not* to have all questions answered; you've decided you can handle the uncertainty. It means you've welcomed Jesus Christ to stand with you and apply His strength to your weakness.[11]

In the three sections below, add to the list depending on the specific "categories" in your life.

For items in the second section, "I'm No Longer Needed by Others," indicate how you've handled each transition (if you've already experienced it) or how you will prepare (if you haven't yet arrived there).

Note your possible or expected thoughts and feelings about each transition in the third section, "I Need Others."

I'm Needed by Others	Children
	Spouse
	Aging parents
	Colleagues
	Neighbors
	Church
	Customers
	Others
I'm No Longer Needed by Others	Empty nest
	Job loss or change
	Retirement
	Church
	Social groups
	Divorce, widower or widow
I Need Others	Physical dependence
	Care receiver
	Retirement home or nursing home[12]

Perhaps you've attended the theater to see a play, or acted in one, and seen some of the cast performing onstage while the rest of the cast is out of sight. They're standing in what we call the stage's "wings," waiting for the moment when they'll appear. Here's something to ponder: What's standing offstage in the wings of your life, waiting to make its entrance?[13]

You need to respond to this question before you move on to life's next chapter. Again, that process happens throughout our life cycle. Even though our seasons may seem more obvious when we're younger—complete school, obtain a job, get married, begin the family-life process, etc.—and even though they may overlap more as we age, they'll always be a part of life. We can resist them or embrace them, but they come and keep coming.

As you consider transitions, then, ask yourself: *What's it time to let go of, or start letting go of, at this point?* Maybe you've been thinking about this already. Perhaps you'd prefer not to face it—it could seem painful or even undoable. However, you may need to respond to this question in order to jump-start or birth a transition that must unfold. The thing that needs changing, or needs to be released, might be something that served you well in its time but doesn't have a future, or it's not what you need in the future.

Would you commit yourself to reflecting on this question for five minutes a day, for one week?

In the privacy of your room, speaking out loud, ask God for an answer to this question. Sit in silence. Listen to Him.

Also, ask a trusted friend to think about this question in regard to you and to give honest suggestions as feedback.

Another thing: Transitions are opportunities to apply our faith. As David Morley notes,

> The change that is so threatening to the nonbeliever is an opportunity for the Christian to exercise his faith and to experience the process of true Christian maturity. The mature Christian is a person who can deal with change. He can accept all of the vicissitudes of life and not deny or complain about them. He sees them all as the manifestations of God's love. If God loves me, then He is going to provide an experience that makes life richer and more in line with His will. To the Christian, "All things work together for good to them that love God" (Romans 8:28). How often we hear that Scripture quoted. How little we see it applied to real-life experiences. What God is really saying is that we should comfort ourselves with the thought that what happens in our lives, victory or defeat, wealth or poverty, sickness or death, all are indications of God's love and His interest in the design of our lives. If He brings sickness to us, we should be joyful for the opportunity to turn to Him more completely.

So often in the bloom of health we forget to remember the God who has provided that health. When we are in a position of weakness, we are more likely to acknowledge His strength, we are more likely to ask His guidance every step of the way.[14]

2

We, the Boomers

My English, German, and Native American ancestors were part of the diverse collection of peoples who had a hand in forming our country. For quite some time, Americans commonly were known or grouped by our background of nationalities; even cities often were characterized by ethnic clusters. Today, whether accurate or otherwise, generational "labels" are more prevalent.

I don't especially like generalizations when it comes to individuals or groups. Nevertheless, one label widely used to characterize a substantial number of people is *baby boomer*, which refers to the population-boom generation born after World War II.

The war ended, the servicemen returned, and, after about nine months had passed since V-day, Americans welcomed more than 230,000 babies in one month! From then until the mid-1960s, about four million children were born annually. In less than two decades, the nation's population increased by more than seventy million, an overall growth, through births alone, of more than 50 percent.

Broadly, baby boomers are those who were born in the United States, Canada, New Zealand, or Australia between 1946 and 1964 (when the first of the boomers already were getting married). Currently, in the U.S., they compose about a fourth of the population. The first generation to grow up with TV, they're likewise the largest and wealthiest generation we've produced.

While another American turns fifty every eight seconds, those born in the mid-1940s are passing their midsixties. Boomers are becoming senior citizens! Approximately thirty-five million Americans already are age sixty-five or older; in fewer than twenty years more than seventy million will be.

Their characteristics have included a determination to *do* something about our world—in one expression, to leave it in better shape than they found it. They've tended to look inward for both strength and solutions. They've been considered flexible and changeable in terms of ideas while displaying resistance toward traditions; their loyalty, historically, was to innovation and individualism rather than to organizations or institutions. This was the first generation whose careers did not remain stable—some due to choice and others to the fluctuating and evolving job market.

Baby boomers have had a major impact upon our culture, and they'll continue to do so during the stage we call retirement—which some have even said they're reinventing. They're well educated, and many have a strong sense of purpose that sustains their desire to make a difference. In this vein, C. S. Lewis said, "Humanity does not pass through phases as a train passes through stations. Being alive, it has the privilege of always moving yet never leaving anything behind. Whatever we have been in some sort we still are."[1]

The Ways We Were

The classic "early boomers," born before 1957, were profoundly influenced by events of the sixties and seventies, especially the Vietnam War and the era's social upheaval. They were consummately idealistic and easily disappointed; they wanted relevance; they sought meaning; they showed intolerance for mediocrity. They also asked, "What's in it for me?" and tended to focus on themselves. Their values had substantial impact on churches (especially worship style), family life, and economics.

Boomers enjoyed being actively involved and tended to avoid passive endeavors—they preferred accomplishment and interaction to spectatorship and isolation. In general, they were accepting in terms of social diversity and personal choice in ways that would easily shock their parents and grandparents. Concerning religion, lifestyle, politics, and more, they tended to think people should be free to believe and live simply as they wished.

Above all, boomers perhaps are most prominently stereotyped with two traits: lack of commitment (e.g., in regard to marriage and family) and focus on instant solutions (e.g., fast food, one-hour cleaners, TV shows that solve all problems in sixty minutes). One frequent criticism has been that, more than anything else, they seem committed exclusively to themselves;[2] that, in the end, their mantra that combines high expectations with short-term thinking (and virtually eliminates concepts like "sacrificing" and "savings"[3]) boils down to "I want it now, I deserve it now, and I'll get it now."

Couples in premarital counseling frequently express such sentiments. When I ask them to write out their life goals, pertaining to different stages, I discover that many want to start at their parents' economic level, even though their parents spent decades attaining that standard of living. They also commonly expect to retire at fifty with sufficient money to do as they wish.

With marriage, though, it's not so much that boomers disliked it as that they had extreme difficulty making it work for a lifetime. They usually defined "traditional family" quite differently than the previous generation: two wage earners with one or two children cared for outside the home during the day. They accepted unmarried cohabitation as well as the universal right to have children, remain childless, have abortions, and/or delay childbearing many years. They were more accepting of same-sex relationships, opposite-sex roommates in the same household, and adoption by a single person or same-sex couple. Over time, the blended family would become the norm.

Broadly, and uniquely, baby boomers had the opportunity to be raised in homes characterized by four potent "E" factors. Though some aspects have changed in the years since, these elements continue to have profound impact.

Entitlement. Parents of boomer children gave them what they wanted. Thus they felt entitled to the best for themselves and their own children.

Entertainment. The now ever-present medium of TV heavily influenced what boomers expected elsewhere, including at school and at church. It also affected their reading ability and diminished their interest in other recreational options. They seized the prerogative to receive enjoyment in life.

Enlightenment. Boomers came to believe they could know and have (and keep) it all. They perceived there was no limit to information, or knowledge, and that they should and could have access to everything. Some parents pushed their children hard and fast to acquire it.[4]

Enchantment. Boomers were enraptured by independence. In many families, the erstwhile value of conformity was overtaken

34

or replaced by the romance of prioritizing self-reliance. That shift, unfortunately, tended to create isolated individuals.

Entering the second half of the twentieth century, America seemed like a car rolling downhill, quickly picking up speed without even a toe on the brakes. The rate of change in every area of life grew rapidly. Not a full generation removed from the Great Depression, and on the heels of the Second World War, most people wanted to savor life and to consume.

About 60 percent of all families would enjoy a middle-class income level and obtain easy credit without major debt concerns. Much more fun than saving was spending, and Americans rushed to gratify their wants, especially with consumer goods. A suburban house with two cars in the garage became the standard. For many, the assembly line was replaced by corporate life.

Parents indulged their kids with "stuff" and in a sense used their possessions to compete with others, measuring their own status in terms of what their children had. Of course the expected outcome was the actual one, as many children came to expect and demand all the more.

However, while kids had loads of material things and plenty of opportunities, in many ways they felt emotionally abandoned. Though they were taught to acquire and accumulate, they weren't shown how to give to or care for others. Our society has most particularly felt the outcome of this during the most recent two decades.[5]

Further, more and more the natural spontaneity of childhood was usurped by constant planned activities. Parents lost the concern for helping their kids develop unique individuality. Socialization, "getting along with others at all costs," was reinforced in the schools, and education was accelerated when Russia launched *Sputnik I* in 1957.

I remember standing outside our Westmont College dorm one night, my friends and I searching the skies for a glimpse of that first satellite. Little did we know how much that event would shape our world. Do you see tumultuous results from the fifties anywhere in your life? In your family? How are your values now different from the ones that typified those years?

Many of us would like to just *forget* the sixties! At that time I was a youth pastor working with several hundred adolescent boomers. The children of the previous decade were growing up and becoming adults; American values were in upheaval.

The fifties even came to seem a window of relative stability in view of the new theme (and pace) of change. The mass media was transforming the world through the discovery and revelation of cultural and political inconsistencies and discrepancies. Those who were completing (or had already established) their values were disillusioned by what they perceived to be widespread hypocrisy and untruth.[6]

The cause for civil rights surged and gained a foothold. But a young president and other leaders were assassinated before our eyes. A bloody war fought far away fragmented our political and educational systems and polarized countless family members. Violence no longer seemed distant or abstract; it was becoming a part of everyday life.

Older folks who'd waded through the Depression's muddy flats or else sacrificed for their children thereafter often were angered to see how adolescents and young adults were behaving. Many youth, challenging the ethics of hard work and competition, declared the American dream worthless and threw their parents' priorities back into their faces.

Behavior once considered off limits became commonplace. Older folks couldn't fathom or handle the "new" words and actions, and generational gaps began to widen into vast chasms. People of different age groups began to isolate and polarize into factions according to their own values. Seniors started migrating en masse into their own communities and retirement centers.

Whomever that brief portrayal of the past represented, today we're not without our own set of problems. Some are even concerned that we older types will be a drain on our society's way of life. However, think about this:

We ourselves are the best answer to that rumored specter of a flood of aging baby boomers washing over the country, hands ever out for higher Social Security checks and more Medicare payments. Our lives refute the dire warning that seniors, retired to lazy days on the golf course, will suck the country dry. Vivacious boomers simply are not about to sit around and contribute nothing. Consider the results of a survey conducted by Experience Wave, which is a national campaign to provide older Americans with more opportunities to stay engaged in work and volunteering. Its survey of adults fifty or older showed some interesting results:

- A majority (53 percent) says the coming wave of retiring boomers actually will be an asset to society. Not only will they be a pool of skilled workers, they'll also have more free time to dedicate to their communities. (Thirty-five percent say they'll be a major burden by putting a severe strain on programs like Medicare and Social Security.)
- Seventy percent said it's very important to find ways to keep older Americans engaged in society, such as working and volunteering.
- Nearly 60 percent said they themselves plan to do volunteer work.[7]

Back to the Present

What do you want out of life *now*? Regardless of where you've been, what you've done, or who you are, *what do you want now?*

If you want to make a difference at this stage, in your own life and in the life around you, there are a number of questions to consider. One source for some helpful guidelines and ideas to assist your approach to your future is Kay Strom's *The Second-Half Adventure*. Here's a general summary:

What are your skills? What are your job skills, people skills, other skills? Be very specific as you identify them. Some may be what you've learned; some might be innate but as yet undeveloped. Even in our older years we can learn, and our brain can still change.

What are you passionate about? What do you really want to do? Something you've done before? Something you've always desired? How will this be a good fit in terms of what you're capable of doing or learning?

Do you have an adventure goal? (That is, a strong desire and plan for, say, going somewhere or investing in something new.) If so, what would be its purpose? How could you incorporate both your abilities and your passion?

What's your ministry history? Or will this be the first time you have the opportunity to be involved? What can you offer to a ministry in terms of knowledge and abilities? (If you've never considered this, you might find it helpful to talk with your pastor or church board.)

What do you see when you evaluate your physical strengths and limitations? Consider your health challenges now; note whether there are indications of potential challenges in the future. If you have a spouse, think about the same factors for him or her.

If you're married, have your spouse respond to each question also. *Which purposes, desires, emotions, or intentions do you share? Which are different?* For the things you want to do or see or become together, it's vital to support each other and move forward as a team.

To *what extent has prayer played a part in your decision-making?* If prayer has been a pattern in your earlier years, you'll be accustomed to looking outside yourself for guidance and confirmation. If not, it will be part of your new adventure. We can make transitions in our spiritual life as well!

Who in your life can give objective advice, not just confirm what you want to hear? Seek the advice of others! "Plans fail for lack of counsel, but with many advisers they succeed."[8] Encourage those you trust to ask questions that perhaps you haven't considered. Let them know you need straightforward honesty. Ask, for instance, "What are the indications that this will work, and the indications that it might not?" Thank them for their contributions; let them know you'll think about what they've said.

What about finances? What's your situation now, and what does the future seem to hold? What would happen if, say, half of your income no longer existed? Could you do what you're intending to do if you experienced a major financial shift? Are there sufficient funds for your later years, or is downsizing in your future?[9]

As we now examine various phases that are upcoming, have passed, or presently apply, I truly hope the rest of *What's Next?* challenges and guides you to think and do whatever you and God decide for your future—and, once more, that what you determine and do, you will do *wholeheartedly*.

3

The Never-Ending Seasons of Parenting

People usually assume that if we marry, parenting will follow. For most people, it does. Even if you've never experienced this facet of life, though, reading this chapter still might help you understand and relate to those around you whose lives to different degrees have revolved around their children.

When a child is conceived, parents' lives are altered permanently. They begin a brand-new growth process that, frankly, can be very disruptive, for they must relearn *and* recreate their world. The influence of their big addition reaches out in ways never imagined and touches life in ways unplanned for.

Your choices of where to live, when to work, how much time to spend with friends, how you relate to your parents, how you dress, how much money you save and spend, and what you eat and drink—just to name a few aspects of your life—change according to each season of parenthood you experience. In becoming a parent, you embark on a series of transformations. From the moment your child is born to beyond the season when he or she becomes a parent, the influence of parenthood on you—your choices, your priorities, your fears, your sacrifices—never ends until your life ends.[1]

For every person who embarks on the voyage of parenthood, that endeavor becomes, for better or for worse, the single most powerful driving force from that point forward.

If you're a parent, you're probably saying *"Absolutely!"* While you've shaped your kids' lives, they've also played a prominent role in forming yours and have profoundly impacted who you are today. Think about it: How different might your beliefs, your experiences, your schedule, your achievements be if you hadn't had children?

Each child's entrance sets off a series of life-altering events (think about the influence on your sleep, lovemaking, meals, vehicles, vacations, home style and size . . .). Furthermore, when moved from every developmental stage to the next, you were handed yet another set of adjustments (including physical, intellectual, relational, emotional, and spiritual). And there's at least one other factor that plays into who you've become: your age.

Perhaps you'd thought that once your children left and got out on their own, you were done? Surprise! It's just the opposite, for in many ways you *then* begin . . . yes, an entirely new stage of parenting.

Maybe you wondered how others survived parenthood. Maybe you wondered whether anyone else felt like you did. Some parents endure agony and depression when their first-born goes off to college or when the baby of the family leaves home. Others rejoice at the thought of one fewer dependent to take care of or take delight in the freedom of a totally (at last!) empty nest.

Some parents resist an adult child returning home; others welcome him or her with open arms. Perhaps we all carry into our own life messages from our parents' marriage and parenting style. Perhaps many of us tend to replicate the "original" rather than create what *we* really want. Regardless, each family unit will have its own unique features and responses.

Our phases were unique in that while our daughter, Sheryl, followed the expected developmental stages, our son remained a dependent infant for twenty-two years. Matthew was born profoundly retarded (as it was called then) and with brain damage, which led to grand mal seizures. When he died he was less than two years old mentally.

Matthew's influence on us was remarkable, especially in shaping certain character qualities and beliefs. Much of what we normally would have done for a child, we didn't do; the everyday maintenance and care revolved around meeting his basic needs, which dominated our lives for the eleven years he lived at home. During the following eleven years, as I've mentioned, he lived in a home that offered specialty assistance we couldn't give. After he moved to Salem Christian Home, we parented him once a month for a weekend.

Seven years after Matthew left, Sheryl departed for a year at college and then moved out permanently (so we thought). We were thrust into the empty-nest stage seven to ten years ahead of when we thought it would arrive. But then we began to experience the boomerang effect: After eighteen months of just the two of us, Sheryl called and said, "Daddy, wouldn't you and Mother like to have me come home and live with you guys for a while?" I got over my shock, my instant inner response of *no!* and stammered, "Oh . . . oh, you'll have to talk to your mother." I knew it was the coward's way out.

A week later Sheryl returned for several months (with a cat). Her return was more of an adjustment for us than was her leaving when she moved out again (and she left the cat!).

Our sense of relief was short-lived, since over the next four years she returned another three times (once with a second cat we inherited). Clearly we fluctuated back and forth in our family stages, seeming at times to go forward and at other times, in certain ways, to regress.

The last time Sheryl returned was just before her wedding. I still recall her saying, "Wouldn't you like to spend these last three months together so we can enjoy all the wedding preparation details?" Of course, *I* heard, "Daddy, I want to save money!"

Obviously that's only part of the story. When we were done parenting our children, we then were parenting our parents. Both of our mothers were approaching ninety and lived in a nearby retirement community. We were the primary overseers and caregivers until my mother died at ninety-three and my wife's mother died at ninety-five.

Change: You Can Count on It

As for your story, consider these "parental" words. Did you voice them, or some of them? If you didn't, did you want to?

> I felt like a combination chauffeur, ATM and traffic controller. Ever since the children came, everything in my life [has] changed. I knew some of it would, but not this much. My friends said I wasn't the same person. Why didn't someone warn me my life would be transformed to this extent? I thought a parent just, well, you know, *added* parenting to their life and everything else kept on the way it was.
>
> My work schedule has never been the same; our love life was hit-and-miss (and fast!); what I wanted was immaterial; time with friends was dependent on (1) babysitting money; (2) health of kids (are they throwing up again?); (3) availability of babysitter. At times I wondered if it was even worth the hassle.

And our cars! At the stage of BK (Before Kids), we had a snappy little convertible. . . . But now of course our choices were totally dependent upon what was needed for the children. We looked at size, shape, safety features (with or without front or side or ceiling air bags); we pondered DVD players (and how about straitjackets?); we calculated gas mileage from all angles. . . .

I have a friend who's a travel agent. When she described her job to me, I said, "That's no different than what I do each day." I organize trips, schedule departure times, arrange for transportation, and, if I'm not available, I call for reinforcements or find a way to send the kids with someone else.

Each week brings piano lessons for two children; soccer practice for three; soccer games for three (one at 9:00, one at 10:00, and the other at 10:00 at another location—*help!*); Pioneer Girls for two; Cub Scouts for one, orchestra for one; a tutor for one; and these are just the regular ones. There's always something seasonal or surprising: doctor, dentist, shopping, teacher conferences, sign-ups for the next wave of things.

We've felt that if they didn't have these experiences now, they'd be at a disadvantage when they became teenagers. But it all costs money, too. And the clothes and shoes *must* be brand-name. I wish I had more control over my life. Well, someday . . . maybe . . . I'm already looking forward to . . . *WHEN?*

Sound familiar? If not, you're unusual. There's no way around it: When we become parents, our lives change. Our children influence what we do, where we go, and, to some degree, who we become.

Recently I came across a book, *The Eight Seasons of Parenthood*, that's fascinating yet shocking, both insightful and penetrating. It shows how each inevitable stage of our children's lives puts us into a new phase of our adult lives. (Some parents with multiple children are in several stages at once.) I wish every prospective parent had this information ahead of time.[2]

In parenting terms, during the first season—*The Celebrity*—the parent is at the center of attention, given special consideration because of "the baby." You've entered a select group; you're expected to perform in a certain way; everyone's interested in your every move. A prospective mom is discovering how her life is no longer her own. The coming child determines what she eats, what side she sleeps on, how long she can work.

The second season, which began at the birth, was *The Sponge*, and guess why? The infant constantly depends on someone else for maintenance and nurture. Your life was totally controlled, whether or not your infant seemed "high maintenance." You also felt wrung out and drained of all personal resources—you were neglecting your own needs to meet your child's.

Third, when *The Family Manager* season rolled around, the power struggles began, and the issue was "who's in charge." You handled, controlled, or diverted the household resources, expenditures, and schedules. You determined what the children could or couldn't do; you oversaw their training, their performance, their diet, their safety, and so on.

Others looked to you and/or your spouse for information, knowledge, and leadership in matters involving your toddlers or preschoolers. You were supposed to be an expert but probably didn't feel like one, because you weren't. After all, who prepares to be a parent? Most of us spent more time preparing to get our driver's license.

You had the responsibility; everyone *else* wanted the privileges!

Being self-controlled when their offspring gets out of control requires Family Managers to morph into patient and empathic negotiators every day, many times a day. Instead of throwing tantrums themselves, parents must learn how to "make deals" with their little ones when they test their every rule or refuse with fiery defiance being told what to do.[3]

The name of the game now was "Let's Make a Deal," and it *definitely* wasn't a TV show. During that critical time you learned to be a capable, loving trainer. (Perhaps in certain areas you instead slid into patterns of indulging, spoiling, or coddling.)

Fourth, when your children reached the elementary years, you graduated as well—to the position of *The Travel Agent*. Itineraries were a daily concern. You had power and authority to plan, organize, and direct activities—where your children went, what they did, and when they did it. You were their guide and liaison; you wanted them to be safe, comfortable, and accepted by others.

Interfering with a well-planned schedule were the requirements and demands imposed by teachers, friends, coaches, your own children, and others. This isn't a favorite memory for most parents. You wanted your kids to go somewhere and do something they didn't want to do, and they probably wanted you to go somewhere and do something you didn't want to do. The smoothness (or relative chaos) of this time likely depended more on your kids' wants than on their needs.

In the fifth season, could there have been any *more* pressure? The hormonal shifts of adolescence took root, and you, *The Volcano Dweller*, lived on the edge, waiting for eruptions to occur at any and all moments (and without warning). You may have lived in fear of what the volatility would do to you, to other family members, to society at large. You may likewise have feared that you'd failed as a parent. Probably you were challenged in every area of your life. Some parents loved it; others hated it; for those with multiple children this season might have seemed to last forever.

Sixth, *The Family Remodeler* encounters a quiet house (at last) and blank spaces on your calendar. Your babies are out of the nest, and it's time to reconstruct. The three areas in need of refurbishing, known as "The Three I's," are identity, intimacy, and independence.

Your parenting was now limited but no less frustrating. Your child, becoming a young adult, may have been making choices well out of line with your preferences. Letting go was a challenge, and if it once was difficult being needed, you might now have felt mostly or completely unneeded. Conversely, if your child had been hindered in becoming a responsible adult, he or she could have been looking to you for help in all areas (especially financial); in that case, being needed too much would have been the theme of conflicts.[4]

(We'll glance at the seventh "season" in chapter 5 and the eighth in chapter 9.)

Evaluating Your Seasons

Each stage you've experienced carries multiple gains and multiple losses. Regarding the latter, for instance, there's the loss of the constant vitality that the children exuded, the loss of the role of parent, perhaps the loss of a sense of immortality, the loss of being needed, the loss of involvement in kids' lives, the loss of a family structure with its various roles. Many parents struggle with no longer being able to protect their kids or with the realization that they had been the glue holding the marriage together.

Ultimately, the passage of your kids into adulthood involves many emotional factors that can make *letting go* difficult. As one parent said, "I'm afraid I didn't do a good enough job as a parent, and I want more time."

Many lament, "Our family will never be the same." What they're saying is, "The family we had is gone." Though that's true, a new one is being formed, and hopefully it will become one with even greater strengths.

The loss of your family as you knew it occurred gradually, not overnight. Most parents, emotionally and socially, begin that process fairly early on, for letting go is intrinsic to our very role as parents. Some children move slowly into independence; others wrestle it from us as if they're fighting for sustenance in a feeding frenzy. Some start "moving away from home" socially and emotionally well before they're actually, physically leaving. (We'll focus on the empty nest in chapter 5.)

You might be, for one or more reasons, a wounded parent. As I've sat with many, I've heard statements like the following:

"I did something wrong, that's why he's gay."

"I did something wrong, that's why he's using drugs."

"I did something wrong, that's why she's living with that reject."

"I did something wrong, that's why he's schizophrenic."

"I did something wrong, that's why she attempted suicide."

"I did something wrong, that's why he dropped out of school."

"I did something wrong, that's why she has AIDS."

"I did something wrong, that's why he joined a cult."

"I did something wrong, that's why she ran away from home."

We all have dreams for our children. We want them to be happy, well adjusted. We dream that they will be someone important. We dream of their careers, their marriages, their accomplishments. Sometimes we dream dreams for them that are really our unfulfilled dreams. We live our lives over again in them.

We also have more specific expectations for our children. We expect them to follow our morals, our family standards, our dictates regarding grades, behavior and the like. What happens when they do not fulfill our dreams or follow our expectations—if, in fact, they reject our wishes in large part? There can be a kind of loss that is powerful and painful.[5]

If we've become enmeshed in our kids' lives to the point where we have difficulty differentiating between their needs and ours, their wants and ours, even their being and ours, we must start making healthy separations. You'll experience a positive detachment when you recognize that your child is a separate being, and that their taking responsibility is a choice they must make.

When a bee stings, it flies off. The bee itself is gone, and now you have a choice. Leave the stinger in, and the sting will remain painful; it will fester, it may become infected, and you could become sick because of it. Or remove the stinger, and then the pain will last a short time and relatively soon won't be there at all. You'll remember that you were stung by a bee and that it hurt, but healing, as a process, will have taken place.

One of parenting's many goals is moving from the parent-child relationship into the adult-adult relationship. Creating healthy friendships with adult children isn't just necessary, it's also fulfilling.

If you're there now, or if you're approaching this transition, talk with others. Develop a plan so that you're in charge of this time (and not the other way around). Consider and decide what you'll do to handle gains and losses—how you will process your emotions, make adjustments, and move forward.

List what you see as being the actual or potential "benefits" of this stage, then note your possible responses or courses of action.

1. Joy at Ann's calling + departure
2. Joy at Jannie's marriage + faithfulness to us
3. Grief over Karen's horrible decades of suffering and suffering of Matthew, Jack
4. Joy over William's supernatural protection + the return of our love for him
5. Joy at the arrival, so different because I was awake
6. I had prayed for him from early pregnancy because now I was a Christian!
7. still I could be mom even tho the others were grown up and so blessed because he always was my biggest encourager

8.

Identify what you see as being the actual or potential "negatives" of this stage, then indicate your possible responses or courses of action.

1. Bearing a feeling of failure at bringing up Karen right. Suffering depression while trying to be a comforter to William
2. Her abusive spouse + 2 children + fear of her destiny, Matthew's + Jack's destiny but always sure
3. William would be fine somehow.
4. Incredible joy at answered prayer for her + each of the boys — the BIGGEST TEST OF MY FAITH
5. Jesus being so close to me except for the 9 years of separation, doubt + misery when I was
6. depressed. Sickness starting at age 43 that stole "normal" younger years + forced Don to be
7. limited in the life he could have otherwise had.
8. His constant love + support even when I was not "myself" at all.

Being in 50 years of ministry — the later ones in the Secret Place — answers to prayer, learning how to pray according to God's will + knowing I could ask Him for special desires of my heart + He would grant them, when He stood before me, smiled at me + gave me a BIG HUG!

4

Midlife Matters

Midlife can be a time of satisfaction or dissatisfaction. For one thing, some people dwell on their life being half over; others focus on the half that's before them. Either way, hitting middle age can be a struggle. Here are some indications of the turmoil people can experience during this phase.

Dissatisfaction

Of course, dissatisfaction can occur at any time, but in a whole-life sense it's especially common in the middle. Struggles with work, doubts about purpose, strains in the marriage, feelings of being torn between releasing children and helping parents . . . some of these issues surface in ways you haven't experienced before. Life may seem dull or profoundly routine. Some people aren't happy with where they are, where they've been, *or* where they think they're going.

Disorientation

For many, the sense of being discombobulated relates to identity and function. Some perceive that they aren't who they thought they were. The roles they used to fill, the hats they once wore seem irrelevant or unimportant; their identity is shaken as they wonder if what they do really matters—some, for the first time, run into the reality that "who they are" stretches far beyond their responsibilities and roles, and they're uncertain about what they see.

The path to middle age usually had significant markers to guide us along the way, and these gave us security, a sense of direction, some predictability. Now some of the maps we'd been accustomed to following are no longer there. By middle age, our guidance system often seems out of date, and we're faced with the choice of whether we'll be willing to discover and rely on a new model. Uncharted territory is daunting to face and difficult to navigate. We wonder where we're going or even where we *can* go during the remaining time we're allotted.

Discouragement

The abundance of your losses, which unfortunately can include vibrancy and hope, sometimes make discouragement a heavy weight. Paul Tripp said, "It's crushing to wake up to the fact that you long ago put away your satchel of dreams. It's hard to face the fact that you are more cynical than you are expectant."[1]

Dread

As we reconsider our bodies, we can wonder if it's even possible to be positive about aging. Some people feel dread as they experience heightened concerns about weight, diet, aches and pains, and so on.

Disappointment

In the form of general or specific regret, as well as dashed plans and unfulfilled dreams, disappointment like a dark hole seeps into many lives. Twenty years ago you believed it was possible and thought you'd get around to it. Now you don't, and you know you won't.

Disinterest

You can't seem to get motivated, you're missing your old spark . . . disinterest is casting a dark shadow over your life. You wonder if you'll resume caring about work or friends or church or hobbies or God; at best, your passion is on the wane. Maybe you think it's gone.

Distance

It's not uncommon to begin withdrawing to the point where distancing has become a factor. You desire only to be left alone; you feel irritated with people who want to intrude. You'd prefer little (if any) contact with others.

Distraction

If your adherence to long-held values begins to crumble, you might begin feeling or seeming increasingly distracted. There's so much occurring inside you that's troubling; your resistance diminishes, and temptations can begin to seem overwhelming. Some people overeat, others buy, some stray toward unfaithfulness in futile attempts to regain stability.[2]

Modifying the Mind

If you're like me, you've revised some part of your past to an extent. We tend to rewrite it in one way or another, and sometimes what we remember isn't reliably accurate. For those traumatized as children, painful experiences tattooed on their brain are accessed involuntarily. If that happened to you, it could be that the pain of your past is drawing you back.

Painful experiences that weren't traumatic still can act as emotional magnets. For instance, if you have wounds from broken relationships with friends or family members, it could be you never received their acceptance or approval or forgiveness. Or perhaps someone else needs *your* acceptance or approval or forgiveness. Issues like these can fasten their grip upon our mind and be like the bottom of an iceberg, deep and cold and foreboding.

Dan Allender said,

> Memory is to some degree a reconstruction of the past that is highly susceptible to erosion, bias and error. It is a mistake to consider one's memory completely accurate, no matter the level of emotional intensity or detail associated with the memories. We should maintain a tentative, open and non-dogmatic view toward all our memories.[3]

These experiences happened in my seventies . not my middle age

Memories start with an experience, but we often "update" them based on images formed or shaped by the intensity of our emotions. Details are altered, and some parts are reinforced and intensified while others are diminished.

I've heard of family gatherings in which different members share their recollections of their past while others look at one another and mutter, "That's not the way I remember it at all." Distortion can and does occur.

> When we begin to examine our recollections of our past closely, we find that they are malleable. That is not to say that

the original memories are false; but what we thought were the "facts" of our past may turn out to be only a version of what happened to us, a "take" on our experiences . . . which we fixed in our mind long ago. As long as these memories stay fixed, we are locked into an attitude, a general feeling, a guiding image of our past that makes it difficult to make changes. But when we recall and reexamine our memories, we realize just how constructed they are by our guiding image. So they can be deconstructed, and when we do this, our feelings about the past can change also.[4]

Old age when many dear friends have left for heaven

~~Midlife~~ is as good a time as any to begin anew. We have a choice of what to do with a painful past—it needn't keep drawing us back. Memories really don't have a claim upon our present or our future unless we give them permission to have control.

What is it that needs to be repaired or released? Well, I know of very few people who like to be controlled by others, but even memories can dominate us if we let them. There is one way to get loose: it's called forgiveness, of self and of others.

Write a letter of forgiveness to the one who offended or hurt you. You don't have to deliver it (and couldn't, if the person is no longer living), but if you don't, read the letter aloud, alone, and then thank God for His healing in your life. Ask Him to take the burden of the wound or offense from you.

You might also write yourself a letter of forgiveness and then read it aloud, remembering that God knows every thought as well as what we will say before we say it.[5] Thank Him that you're able to forgive yourself and others because of His forgiveness in your life.

Most of us can choose to reconstruct the past in a much more positive way than it occurred. Edit and enhance the best while discarding the worst.

There's an ideal called a balanced mind. While the past, the present, and the future each have a place, it's easy as we get older to let the past have so much room that it crowds out the others. "Aging," someone remarked, "is when we experience fewer and fewer things for the first time and more and more things for the last time." As another suggested, "Aging is when the sum total of our memories exceeds the sum total of our hopes."[6]

You Are Who God Says You Are

One of the not-infrequent responses I've heard at midlife is the word *stuck*.

> I feel stuck. Perhaps I've been stuck in some ways all my life. What I'd like to do and be for the rest of my life is to experience *nothing holding me back*.

Many find themselves at this place in ~~midlife~~ *old age for me*. Why? Sometimes the answer isn't available; sometimes we discover it with a little searching; other times it's obvious. Certain people are immobilized by fear. Others can't find motivation to take the next step. Some won't accept change.

One fifty-year-old said, *when my 1st grandchild was born—the beginning of wonderful years* I feel like a well-used car that was driven in low gear. For some reason we were never able to engage the other gears, so we couldn't get it up to speed. It took forever to get anywhere. Sometimes we never arrived at our destination. *Thank God, not for me*

That's my life. I was never able to engage my life fully, and now I wonder what I missed. I think I avoided looking at my life, who I was and what I did all those years. I was busy. Perhaps one of the reasons I stayed so busy was avoidance.

I thought I was living life, and now, as I reflect back, there was a lot that was unlived. Now I want to live my life as much as possible—to the fullest.

Do you identify with any of this? Consider and answer the following: *no!*

Describe how you have lived life to your fullest. *Family joys to closest to*

Describe how you have not lived your life to the fullest. *very dear friends*

In what way have you not engaged life in the way you've wanted to?

Describe how, in the years remaining, you will live life to the fullest.[7]

In a way, the man mentioned above has found that what he thought worked in the earlier stages of his life perhaps didn't work as well as he thought. Others discover that what did work earlier nevertheless won't work during their later stages.

Achievement wasn't meant to be our driving force or the source of building who we are. We already have an identity, and it has nothing to do with what we're able to produce.

The writers of the Scriptures are careful to point out that when God looks at you in Jesus Christ, He sees you as a brother to His own Son. Because of the work of Christ, all the ugliness of humanity is set aside. God has absolutely no attitude of condemnation toward man. You are worth all of God's attention. If you were the only person in the whole world, it would be worth God's effort to make Himself known to you and to love you. He gives you freely the status and adequacy of an heir to the universe. *I knew this!*

This is agape love, the unmerited, unconditional favor of God for man. We achieve our adequacy through this unceasing love. We do not *become* sufficient, approved or adequate: rather we are *declared to be* such! When we believe this, we become achievers and humanitarians as an effort, a by-product of our new-found selves. *amen*

When a person has accepted adequacy as a gift, he immediately perceives a new standard for achievement. No longer

Mostly
His
faithful —
most to me

does the criterion of human performance apply, but rather the measure of faithfulness judges us. This is the fair standard, the one that stimulates everyone, frustrates no one, and is administered by the providential will of God.[8]

Sometimes one's quest for achievement is justified not toward work but toward "standing" in the church, or spiritual life, yet this doesn't work. Some people try to establish or strengthen their sense of identity through romance, but others weren't meant to be used in this way—no one was designed for that purpose. Neither are parents to get their identity from their kids, but many live vicariously so that what a child achieves or becomes feed into *their* identity.

I've seen parents make major sacrifices for their children, and heard them say it was for the good of the kids, when their fuel was the accolades they received from others for being "sacrificial" and "giving" parents. Their identity was tied into performance and achievement, even though it wasn't their own. What happens if the children fail, or if they don't produce?

> Our children were never given to us to be trophies on the mantel of our identity. If anything, their success is a hymn of praise to another Father who provided everything they need to be where they are and to do what they are doing. As parents we are never more than instruments in his redemptive hands.[9]

When we arrive in middle age and beyond, we've had years to accumulate stuff. For many, moving up is just part of life. In some, the desire for *more* and *bigger* and *better* can be connected to identity.

We feel good about ourselves as we look at what we've acquired. Labels and locations can become important, and, for many people, things begin to define who they are.

Unfortunately, many of these victims of "identity replacement" also fall prey to owing more than they can afford.

We don't need all that we have. We often can't even pay for all that we have. It doesn't satisfy our core needs and desires. It doesn't live up to the claims of what it would do for us. If we base our identity on our stuff, we'll come to discover it was a delusion. Then we'll suffer disillusionment and disappointment.

So much of how we respond to life transitions has to do with what we believe is the source of our identity. One factor in this, especially in our middle years, is called *goal-gap*. This refers to the distance we perceive between the achievements we'd set for ourselves and what we've actually achieved—the gap between what we'd said we'd do and what we've done. A wide gap can affect our self-worth, which in time can impact our emotional life, our spiritual life, and our marriage. Accordingly, we want to ensure that our emphasis is aimed the right way. When, for instance, you believe your career is an end rather than a means to an end, you're setting up shortcomings or failures or disappointments at work to erode or collapse your very identity.

Identity is a major issue for most of us. *Who am I* really is either at the forefront of our thinking or in some way lurking just below the surface. We want to count, and we want to be known.

Years ago I heard a descriptive song:

> If I were a cloud, I'd sit and cry,
> If I were the sun, I'd sit and sigh,
> But I'm not a cloud, nor am I the sun,
> I'm just sitting here, being no one.[10]

No one wants to be "no one," so we strive to be significant. God *wants* us to be productive and to have an impact. But

He never told us to do this in order to determine who we are or establish our significance. He's not calling us to use our accomplishments as the basis for our identity.

Some spend their life hunting each new prize or goal in order to feel *I have value* or *I am someone*. What happens, then, when what we're good at doing diminishes or evaporates? In the midst of disappointment, some will look to God, and for those who do there are two responses.

One response is to blame God for not providing what we desired. Facing losses of any kind, a person's own belief becomes apparent. Many live by their own ideology and interpretation instead of what Scripture teaches.

The other response is the realization that no material thing can satisfy or be our identity source—and that God has something better. An identity built on a spiritual foundation endures, no matter our position or circumstances.[11]

This is the greatest reward Jesus centered others centered

Change Your Outlook, Choose Your Path

Where do you start moving forward in the second half of life? It's simple: *You start at the end.*

That's right. Start at the ending place of where you've been and what you've known.

You'll be in nowhere land for a while. It's difficult to let go of the known and familiar when you don't have a handhold on what's coming. Too many see "nowhere" as merely disruptive and painful; they give in to the fear and focus on the loss. If you instead realize that this is just temporary, you'll move forward. You'll make a difference if you say, "This time can be positive. I *can* handle this. I *will* grow, and I'll enjoy life in a new way."

age 79!

This is called *reframing your perspective*. You take a negative, or what you perceive to be negative, and put it in a different frame, considering and embracing the situation from a different angle with a different focus. Making this change in your thoughts makes it much easier to change your behavior.

So, when you reach midlife (or any other later stage), what primary steps can you take?

First, *recognize the changes taking place.* This involves introspection, self-reflection, taking inventory of what is or seems to be in transition or changing shape.

Second, *acknowledge what these changes represent and why they're occurring.* When you make this admission, then you'll ask and respond to the question "Will I take action, and if so, what kind of action?" (Acknowledging the changes sometimes is an act of resignation, rather than a working toward resolution of the change.)

Third, *think about what response would be best.* Here, if your response is reflective, your progress is likely to be more positive and productive. Too often, the response is reflexive.

There are two basic forms of *reflexive* responses: (1) passive acceptance and (2) active affirmation.

Passive acceptance of change is an easy response for many because their new sense of self is under so much threat. One continues to live as he has, changing neither identity nor actions, and then suffering effects of the change (e.g., depression or erratic behavior). Through passivity he loses much of his excitement, vision, and vitality. He likely suffers and survives in silence.

Others intensify their behavior in trying to actively affirm who they are. They try harder to do what they've been doing for so many years. This helps them thwart the immediate "threat," but it's merely an act of postponement.

The major difference between a reflexive response and a *reflective* response is a difference between resignation/relief and real resolution. After truly recognizing and acknowledging the change, a person's next step is to consider what's going to result from the change and how they can respond and act proactively.

Fourth, *make the choice to change.* Not easy, but straightforward.

Fifth, and finally, *integrate the change.* This is bringing together who you are now with your new choices and actions into a new pattern of life.

The apostle Paul directs

> Do not conform any longer to the pattern of this world, but be conformed by the renewing of your mind. Then you will be able to test and approve what God's will is—his good, pleasing and perfect will.[12]

Want to be your own person at this stage of life? Most do, but most of us, instead of creating who we want to be, allow ourselves to be shaped and conformed by society, which says that we're

- to *be* something
- to *do* something
- to *prove* something
- to *own* something
- to *achieve* something.

All these imply we have to be successful to be acceptable. But who sets the criteria for success? We can follow society's standards, or we can follow God's. Society says take more, make more, spend more, and, above all, get more! And sometimes we equate God's blessings with affluence. However, this is precisely what, in midlife, many begin to question.

It's easy to get caught up in the *wants* and the *shoulds.* Go back to those definitions of societal success (above) and ask: "Who do I want to be? What do I want to do? What do I want to prove? What do I want to own? What do I want to achieve? How can all of this be done God's way, wholeheartedly?"

You don't have to *do*, *prove*, *own*, or *achieve* anything. Jesus Christ has done all of this for you. So relax. Jesus asks you to follow Him, to let Him live His life through you and therefore be who He created you to be.[13]

> Seek first [your heavenly Father's] kingdom
> and his righteousness,
> and all these things will be given to you as well.[14]

5

"The Empty Nest," or "The Emergence"?

I miss the early years with my children. I was so tied up in work during that time."

"They're certainly taking their time moving out. The nest isn't emptying as fast as I want."

"I looked at that small chair and started to cry. It seemed like just yesterday my son was sitting in it."

"I'm sure I'll be glad when they've left. But won't I feel useless?"

"That room seems so empty since he's been gone."

"I'm looking forward to a new job—this time, for *pay!*"

"Now it's only the two of us. And . . . we sit. We don't talk. We don't look at each other. *Nothing.*"

"Parenting is hard work, and I can hardly wait to give my two weeks' notice."

"We married at twenty and had the first one at twenty-two. The last one came at thirty-four. He left when he turned twenty-one. No one mentioned—and we didn't dream—that it would take a third of a *century* before we'd be alone again as a couple."

"We're already well adjusted to our new reality. I hope none of them divorces or loses a job . . . we like this setup!"

"I don't want to build my happiness on when they call, write, or visit. I need to have my own life."

"They left too quickly, married too young, and had kids too soon. They need to realize I'm not their on-call babysitter. I raised one family; I'm not raising another."

"I've done what I could. They're in the Lord's hands now. And I guess they always have been, come to think of it."

Two of my friends described their progression into and through the empty-nest stages as similar to Moses leading the children of Israel into the wilderness—after Egypt, before the Promised Land. During their season of "wandering," they said it had been "so different. So quiet. So strange. We looked forward to it *and* dreaded it at the same time. Maybe it would have been easier, somehow, if it had been one or the other."

There's the missing noise, the dearth of activity, the absence of tension (sometimes). The bedrooms are empty, and sometimes the schedule seems vacant too. While the meals and laundry get scaled down, some people feel their purpose and their passion have shrunken or diminished also.

Reactions, transitions, and adjustments vary widely. Some look back and think they did a good job. Others are filled with regrets and a pervasive sense of failure. Many experience a mixture of both, and more. The language used to describe this phase, however, almost always conveys a negative impression.

"The empty nest" connotes an aura of sadness, a hint of uselessness, even an indication that one's function is finished. Who says, though, that we can't consider this season as, for instance, "the second honeymoon," or "the freedom stage," or "the opportunity for reawakening," or "the next growth phase," or "the emergence"? Yes, there is loss—and we needn't pretend otherwise—but this likewise is a time of gains. The empty nest doesn't have to be a crisis; honestly, it's a passageway between two eras in a parent's life.

For some couples the empty nest *is* a crisis, perhaps a mingling of at least as many feelings as expressed in Ecclesiastes 3:1–8 (a time of weeping, laughing, mourning, healing, loving, releasing, losing, embracing, and more). You might feel sadness as you realize one cherished life facet or another is now about memories of the past rather than circumstances in the present. Even so, above all, this can be a time of celebration and of hope. This time of apparent endings really is about beginnings. *Our 80's:*

This stage isn't summed up by "closing doors" or "letting go." There's great potential for new experiences, for adventure. You might be freer to set your own pace and to plan your own schedule. You can forge pathways to personal growth, to relational investments, to interests and hobbies, perhaps to travel or a new career, to a stronger, deeper, better marriage.

Serious physical limitations have definately had to be factored in with the above

Parents in Process

Here's part of one father's experience:

> When our third child went off to college, there was a strange silence in the home. It was quiet. It was eerie. I wandered around the place. I wasn't doing all the things I had done for years, and neither was June. It was scary.
>
> I had the time for myself that I'd always hoped for, but there was nothing to fill it. It didn't feel right. I didn't have any of the kids to check up on or to interact with or go somewhere with. I didn't feel needed anymore. I realized I wasn't a father anymore . . . yes, I was a father, but I didn't do "fathering," and June didn't do "mothering."

Here I was, not knowing what to do to fill all the fathering time. At first I had this sense of fear, but fortunately it turned into freedom. It's okay that the kids don't need me the way they used to need me. There's more time for June and me and more money for us. We've had to get used to the changes in the kids, but they have to get used to the changes in us, too.

If both mother and father respond in this way, they can experience a time of positive growth individually and in their marriage. If, for example, the mother is struggling with her loss of identity, having been over-involved with her children, she may be prone to spend her energy attempting to reconnect or to stay enmeshed, and a distancing may occur in their marriage.

Again, some mothers are relieved at moving beyond everyday parenting experiences; others loathe the silence in the home and acutely feel a lack of usefulness. Some feel that part of them is slowly dying as they struggle to come to grips with "that was then, and it's no longer here." Mothers who struggle the most are those who feel their children didn't turn out the way they wanted, or didn't live up to their expectations.[1]

Feeling disenchantment or disorientation is a healthy sign that shows you're moving toward transition. You may feel scared or unnerved for a while, and this too is normal for the ending of part of your life. You're in a "who am I" stage— it's all right to feel as though you were cut adrift. Pray and meditate, and ask for direction, guidance, and patience as you pray. Taking your time means you're taking the time to grow during this unsettling phase.

I've found that a midlife woman's adjustment to the empty nest is based on a number of factors:

- How far away her grown children live and how often she sees them (the farther away, the more difficult the adjustment).

- The quality of relationships between her and the children. (If it's strong, she'll undergo adjustments in the frequency and quality of contacts. If shaky, the relationships themselves can be threatened.)

- How successful she feels at having fulfilled her role as parent. (Guilt might rear its head now.)

- How many roles she currently identifies with. (Generally, the more roles, the better.)

- The quality of her marriage. (If the children were used as a buffer, she may have intense concern about how to go about putting back vitality into a devitalized relationship.)

- Her adaptability; how well she handled previous stresses and changes; how able and willing she is to roll with the punches.

- Early experiences in her family of origin. (How she and her parents responded at the time of her departure can greatly influence her current response.[2])

The authors of *Loving Midlife Marriage* describe a number of different mothering styles. An *eternal* mother, for instance, continues with a child-centered life, responding to the kids as if they were still living in the home, living for and through her children. The offspring face difficulty in separating and attaining individual growth.

A *mourner* mother moves on with life but responds as if she's going through the motions. Her contacts are infrequent; her regrets and if-onlys are prevalent. A *relieved* mother moves on, focusing upon her own growth and sometimes also on her marriage.

Grievers do just that: They work through relinquishing their kids, and they move on. They discover new roles; some are career-driven. Basically, they're happy, they're well adjusted, and often they have strong marriages.[3]

One midlife transition that occurs especially after the children leave is the switching of roles. The rules by which you play the game may have changed or be changing as well. Gail Sheehy, a pioneer researcher, wrote:

> A massive shift takes place across gender lines as we grow older. What is observable empirically is that women begin to be more focused, more interested in tasks and accomplishments than in nurturing, whereas men start to show greater interest in nurturing and being nurtured. . . . Women become more independent and assertive, men more expressive and emotionally responsive. These changes in middle and later life are developmental, not circumstantial, and they occur in predictable sequences across widely disparate cultures.[4]

Heeding Signs of Warning

The responses of men are as varied as their family circumstances. The loss of the father role as he's known it can lead to depression and not only "What do I do now?" but even "Who am I now?" One said,

> I knew they would leave at some time. That's not the shock. I knew there would be adjustments and changes. I knew our relationship would change and that I wouldn't be called on as much anymore. . . . [Yet] I didn't realize I would be so different. They're grown up and on their own, but I feel as though they took the best part of me with them.

Some fathers try to hold on to their role at any cost; some begin reacting negatively toward younger people in general; some seek out younger people who will allow them to act as a father figure or father type. Others feel the loss but also feel a sense of relief as their fathering responsibilities diminish, seeing open doors to invest time and energy elsewhere.

As the home atmosphere drastically changes, there are fewer choices to make. Old habit patterns, especially of time usage, won't apply, and new pressures may surface. Needs formerly filled by children—such as communication, affection, and companionship—will be diverted to someone else for fulfillment. If couples rush at each other, demanding that he or she replace previous interaction with a child, they may push each other away.

One danger that can creep in at this stage, though, is when one or both spouses replace their presence not with more time and focus on each other, together, but in seeking to fill the empty space by latching on to things and activities. There's certainly more effort and risk with endeavoring to connect in positive new ways with your spouse than with habits and hobbies.

Many studies show that the last child's leaving brings an increased likelihood of marital maladjustment. This event acts as a catalyst, requiring that husband and wife face themselves, each other, and their marriage in a new way. The longer they avoid it, the faster the gap between them widens.

There ought to be a sign given to parents at the very start that says "Parenting Can Be Hazardous to Your Marriage." It needn't be, since they can nourish their relationship even as they raise children, but for many it's neglected. If the marital relationship had been fragile, there's a risk that now it will disintegrate. Some even feel they now have paid their dues and can end a union in which one or both perceive the kids to have been holding it together (especially if the mending seems more work than it's worth).

The mother who's devoted herself almost entirely to her children can feel abandoned and unloved when they leave. Seeing herself as having joined the ranks of the unemployed, she may begin to feel that there's little reason or justification for her life, that she has little to contribute. She may experience depression and share the feeling of the mother who said she "felt like dying" when her last daughter married.[5]

> Many parents see their children as extensions of themselves, or as their possessions, or as the fulfillment of their unfulfilled lives. These are all potentially destructive attitudes to have toward raising one's children. All of these "beliefs" make children into "little idols" in one form or another. We "idolize" them. We hallow them and their achievements. We have to, because we have invested so much of ourselves in them. Such idolatry, created by unresolved grief, not only blocks grieving, but blocks the opportunity to discover our children as adults.
>
> The central theological question is: "Whom do our children belong to?" For people of faith, the answer should be: God. Isn't that what we acknowledge in infant baptism or dedication? God gives them to us as gifts. They are on loan. Our job is to raise them, teach them, love them and then launch them into the world, thereby returning them to God. They are only with us for a short time.[6]

Think of a child's growth in concert with words from our nation's Declaration of Independence, which is something that happens "in the course of human events." Since it's inevitable, we'd be better off to prepare for it and foster it. As much as possible, parents need to oversee and facilitate the process rather than have a family fragmented as its members break away.

When parents don't let go, the whole family can face dire consequences: Thank you Lord for not allowing this to happen with us. We poured in lives into our spiritual family

It leaves emotionally crippled parents living their lives through emotionally crippled children who then feebly try to perform as adults while avoiding the responsibilities of determining the destiny of their life, offspring and society. The results are a loss of independence for all—past, present and future.[7]

Letting Go on the Plateau

The biggest empty-nest step is summed up in two words: *Let go*. Regardless of how your children turned out, hanging on is detrimental to everyone. This is the time to identify your expectations for them and perhaps make some adjustments.

It may be helpful to consider how you separated from your family when you established being on your own. Do you remember what you did and how you felt? Did your parents release you and encourage you to move on, or did they cling to you in some way? Did you or they go through a grieving process during the transition? Can you remember your (and your parents') emotions from that time? Often people have a mixture of feelings, in which part of them is expectant and part is reluctant. In what way did you experience this? How did your parents assist you and/or hinder your moving on? What did you learn that you used or didn't use (or will/won't use) in the releasing of your kids?[8]

I read the story of a mother who was struggling with letting go and adjusting to the empty nest. She had an assignment in a creativity class to make a collage, so she decided to have it reflect her life transition. She took copied photos of her daughter's high school graduation pictures and cut them into pieces—eyes, chin, mouth, nose, etc. The week before, she'd drawn a self-portrait that depicted her sadness; she cut that into pieces as well. On a paper background, she glued the features together into their respective general areas and connected the features with jagged, irregular lines. The result was an image of chaos—each component was a part of the other but also separate. It described an old identity in the process of change at the same time a new one was emerging. So it is, in some way, for every parent going through this stage.

Gerald Kierman of the Harvard Medical School says the departure of grown children often necessitates major renegotiation of the marriage relationship. Suddenly the couple is thrown together alone, no one else to talk to. Though the empty-nest syndrome is described as a maternal issue, the father can suffer greatly when the last teenager cleans out his closet and takes down his posters. The daughter who was Mommy's little girl at six has become Daddy's special pal; when she goes, he's devastated.[9]

The empty-nest experience can bring a devastating sense of emptiness and purposelessness. Loneliness can land. A silent house full of memories. There was once so much to do, and now, seemingly, there's so little. The crowded, busy years seemed arduous at the time, but, looking back, it's clear that was far outweighed by the deep, solid satisfaction of being needed.[10]

If you are not yet an empty nester or a retiree, imagine that you've already moved into your new role. Now ask yourself the following questions. You may want to write your answers in your journal.

How have the children affected us positively?
How have the children affected us negatively?
What activities am I engaging in? How do I feel [when I'm] doing them? Is there something more I would like to do?
What people are involved in my life now? What part do they play?
What is our relationship like now? What are we doing to enjoy ourselves? What problems are we having in the marriage?
What would my ideal day look like as an empty nester?[11]

Perhaps we're talking about you at this point. If you've had children, it's either facing you in the future, you're there now, or you've moved on. This stage frequently involves four generations: you, (your elderly parents,) your children, and your grandchildren. (If you have no grandkids, you may *and your great grandchildren!*

have a rare level of independence.) Your parenting might not have *stopped* but rather *shifted* to your parents; one of them could end up living with you. You'll learn from your children how to live life in new ways, some of which you may not agree with, and from your parents you may learn how to die.

There's a term for people at this stage:

Plateau Parents are the lighthouses, the beacons of the family, perched atop a plateau on the mountain of parenthood that you've been climbing for over two decades. You've now completed the remodeling of your family, enabling your children to feel comfortable returning to the empty nest as self-sufficient and responsible adults who have created an independent life of their own.

You're ready for a time of rest and relaxation, a time to finally say that the first circle of parenthood, parenting children, is officially over and the second circle, parenting adults, is officially in gear. You can bask in the glow of your fully grown children, the "fruits" of all your previous parenthood labors. The remodeled family, whatever its shape and size, is the central magnet pulling you as Plateau Parents in one direction or another on your mountaintop perch.[12]

Progressing Proactively

Regardless of your circumstances, this time of your life will not be problem-free. Conflicts will arise—for example, between what you dreamed of doing and the presence of your grandchildren. When your kids are really launched, it's time to look at decisions that may have been put on hold.

Do I want to stay in this career or not?

Do I want to retire early?

Do I want to go back to work?

What new hobbies do I want to take up?

Should we move, downsize, or buy a fifth-wheel and travel?

One couple said, "When the house was empty, for the first time in forty years we 'got a life' again. We had to practice saying no to our kids when it came to being their babysitter. We had to establish new boundaries and new rules. But it is working."

Some parents want as much involvement with grandchildren as possible, for once again they're needed. Some even see a second chance to make up for what they "didn't do right" the first time. I've talked with a number of younger parents, though, who were apprehensive about their parents' involvement with *their* children. They carried emotional wounds and in some cases trauma from their childhood. Some were concerned about how heavy-handed their parents had been and might still be with their own children.

Further, what happens if one of you wants this involvement and the other is more interested in new freedom? Every grandparent needs to ask, "Who would I be and what would I do if I didn't have grandchildren?" Again, too, in addition to the grandchildren, their own parents may now need to be parented.

There are many who see grandparenting as giving them new meaning, another opportunity to give and influence others as well as to be needed. Others find purpose in giving support and meaning to their own parents. So much of what happens is based upon our attitude as well as how we view "old age." How you look at and talk about the future may determine how you live out your remaining years.

How the rest of your life will be is your decision. You do have choices. If you have healthy adult-to-adult relationships with your now-independent children as well as with your parents, you'll be able to offer much experience.

Many parents reach the empty-nest stage well past midlife, even close to retirement. Those with several children might see the oldest presenting them with grandchildren before their last child leaves. Many have to juggle their kids at different stages and never fully get to that place where it's "just the two of us again." The increase in blended families has meant that, for many, some of the stages seem endless or even endlessly repeated. Personally, I became a widower at seventy, with one six-year-old grandchild; three years later I'd accumulated six more between ages two and eighteen!

I'm sure you've heard the word *proactive.* In a sense it can mean taking charge of an upcoming or future event instead of letting it overwhelm you. I read the suggestion of creating a ritual to mark the passage of the empty nest, to yield a sense of predictability and control that can ease transition. It can bring meaning into pain and help us move on to the next event or transition.

Some parents go through all the children's pictures, or make a collage of them, or view all the videos, or write good-bye letters and then either read or sing them out loud, together, and give them to the children. You could also

- assemble objects that represent the highlights of the years spent with your children as they were growing: photos, toys, clothing, videos, certificates, artwork, gifts. The list is endless.

- plant a new tree at each child's departure, together, and watch the trees (and your children) grow;

- invite friends and loved ones to your home to talk about the time spent with your children during their years there;

- individually, write about your memories and your current desires. Read them aloud to each other.

Finally, many rituals possess these elements:

1. *Creating an atmosphere.* Think about the setting in which you'll perform your ritual (e.g., indoors or out? Day or night?).

2. *Performing healing acts.* Think about:
   - What is it that you experienced over the years with your children, their meaning in your life/lives?
   - What has changed as or since they've grown?
   - What do you want to accomplish now? What do you want for your life/lives as individuals and as a couple? What do you want for your relationship with your grown children?

3. *Releasing, giving thanks, and letting go.* This step allows you to acknowledge all that's gone before; to appreciate what you've had with your children; to look forward to what you want for yourself as well as your relationships with them. "Letting go with love" is apt here, for the more positive this step, the better the outcome for all.

The way in which you perform this step is also quite personal:
   - You might say something to the effect of "I'm letting go."
   - You could write about releasing the ties.
   - You might think about it, sing about it, dance about it.
   - You may blow out the candles or watch them burning down.[13]

6

The Second Half of Marriage

Marriage is never complete. It's never static. Changes or flux are the only constant, whether or not you're aware of it.

It's ever in process. If you said each morning, "What will be different in our relationship today?" and then looked, you'd discover. No marriage really stagnates—it's moving either forward or backward.

Midlife can be a time of reminiscence, a time of growth, a time of challenge, a time of delight . . . *a time to welcome.*

For some couples this is a reality. But for others midlife is about crisis. There's turmoil in the marriage resulting from personal changes taking place within husband or wife or both.

At middle age the "normal" defects in any relationship seem to show up in sharper focus. There's now more time to notice and confront. The couple can't relocate the buffer of romance and passion that characterized their earlier years, an adhesive that's very much needed yet seemingly so difficult to regenerate. They're faced with getting older; the threat of aging is painful.

This crisis point is also the time for what Ken Kesey described in *Sometimes a Great Nation* as the "go-away-closer disease." The husband or wife may be starving for contact but avoids it like poison when it's offered. He or she may long for human connection but sabotages any chance for it to happen. He or she may erect barriers to keep the other from getting too near, too intimate, too involved—yet he or she is unhappy and restless in isolation.

How do you catch this strange illness? It seems to come in varying degrees along with "middlescent malaise." The frustration or disappointment we feel about the world and what it's done for us (or prevented us from doing) is directed at the one with whom we live in closest proximity. It's another form of "kicking the cat." We may sense that things have gone awry, but for some reason we find it impossible to talk about the situation with our spouse. Eventually we stop ourselves from caring about or doing as much for him or her because our own problems require all of our attention.

Middle age and the empty nest can bring major changes in numerous areas. Also major *choices*. One is this: You can preserve the best from the years of your marriage up to now and discard the worst of the experiences. Or you can continue to cultivate the worst and ignore the positives and see it deteriorate. Too many live with the residue of early marital disappointments and have allowed those to destructively determine and dictate the future.

Creating the Right Marriage

Years ago I found a statement that reflects good thinking. It said that while at first married people were concerned about meeting the "right one," now we're learning the importance of *being* the "right one" for someone else.

If you treat the wrong person like the right person, you may have married the so-called "right person" after all. If you treat the right person like the wrong person, that's most likely who you married. And it *is* far more important to be the right person than it is to marry the right one. In short, *whether you married the right or wrong person is primarily up to you.* How you're treating her (or him) makes all the difference.

Regardless of why you married, the fact remains: you did, and you are. Every couple encounters surprises. We can either allow those to totally throw us or we can use them as growth opportunities and make adjustments. Reality sets in after the wedding, but don't think of it as being synonymous with trouble or disappointment. Instead, see and embrace the potential for making new discoveries, for developing flexibility and protection against stagnation within the relationship— even if you've been married for decades.

In some sense, too, we all choose a "wrong person" to marry, because there's something wrong with all of us. We're created in God's image, but at the same time we're afflicted with a fatal condition. Our having been born sinful has become politically incorrect, but the evidence is too strong to ignore. We are flawed. We are broken. We all are "wrong people."

Blunt as this is, we're all then confronted with its truth. What you're facing in the remaining years of your marriage may seem like an uncharted journey. However, for many today the second half of marriage may be longer than the first! Decide what you *want* and intend to *do* at this stage.

It's not just your marriage facing you, either, but all the new adjustments, each of which can affect your marriage: Your children are leaving or have left the nest, or they've stayed around too long, or they were out and have returned and perhaps with their own children. Your parents are aging or have aged to where you will be or are parenting them. Guess who else is aging, and how will that affect what you'll be able to do? Then throw in retirement and your later years. Two friends of mine described the choices well:

> Are you willing to take the risk to grow together in your marriage so the second half is far better than the first half? It may involve making yourself more vulnerable to your spouse and disclosing yourself in a deeper way. Or it may involve rearranging your schedule, learning new skills or changing some of your personal habits. But if you want to have a more personal and satisfying relationship with your spouse for the second half of marriage, we encourage you to take the challenge seriously.[1]

Change does bring disruption. Even if we do like it, still it's going to be uncomfortable, and we may try to resist the process. You might even become angry with your spouse for changing in a direction you appreciate! In many such cases it's not their behavior that triggers your reaction but your own thoughts about the behavior. For many, it's fear of what change may mean to *their* life.

Your marriage is a lifelong adventure with highs, lows, and detours. Every journey is unique—no two couples travel one road. Some experience marriage without giving it much thought, while others constantly take their marital temperature. Some underrate marriage and only see the problem, what isn't there. Others view marriage through blinders and are oblivious to issues that eat away at its core.

Your marriage is like a car that every now and then needs a tune-up. Often, when your car's getting tuned up, the mechanic finds the beginning of a problem and takes corrective action to minimize damage. If you neglected this service, something could break and result in a major overhaul that would be more expensive, time-consuming, and disruptive.

Assessing your marriage, you may discover the seeds or new growth of a problem that had been hidden like termites in a building's foundation. Now you have a head start on taking corrective action. Seize that opportunity!

Many neglect this servicing, to destructive effect. Many married couples realize in midlife or in their later years that their neglect had made their excursion unpleasant (or worse).

Before ever starting out on a long trip, a wise driver will try to determine what he's most likely to encounter along the way. How are the roads? Will there be detours? What's the weather report? And so on. Ascertaining some of these answers ahead of time will better prepare him if or when he gets to where his progress could be hampered.

Life itself likewise has a beginning and some type of conclusion. Its events follow a basic sequence and progression: sometimes smooth and orderly, sometimes rough and bumpy. Its stages or periods might be called *seasons*; the Bible says, "To every thing there is a season."[2]

Daniel Levinson spoke about this:

> There are qualitatively different seasons, each having its own distinctive character. Every season is different from those that precede and follow it, though it also has much in common with them. The imagery of seasons takes many forms. There are seasons in the year: spring a time of blossoming, winter a time of death, but also a rebirth and the start of a new cycle. There are seasons, too, with a single day—daybreak, noon, dusk, the quiet dark of night—each having its diurnal, atmospheric and psychological character. There are seasons in a love relationship, in war, politics, artistic creations and illness.

Metaphorically, everyone understands the connections between the seasons of the year and the seasons of the human life cycle. No one needs an explanation of the lyrics to "September Song." When the hero sings, "It's a long, long while from May to December/And the days grow short when you reach September," we all know that he is referring to the contrast between youth and middle age. When Dylan Thomas in his celebrated poem tells his aging father, "Do not go gentle into the good night," it is clear to all that the coming of night is experienced as the end of life.

To speak of seasons is to say that the life course has a certain shape, that it evolves through a series of definable forms. A season is a relatively stable segment of the total cycle. Summer has a character different from that of winter; twilight is different from sunrise.[3]

Just as we have individual seasons, so are there seasons in a marriage. To know these phases of development ahead of time is to be prepared for them.

Whether you've been married a few years or fifty, there's one ingredient that holds your marriage together. Not love. It's commitment. One man said,

> I think some transitions take much longer than others. Here, I'm thinking of the joy that comes from my being in a long-term marriage of committed companionship that has evolved over many decades. The joy here, I think, comes from knowing that the hard work, disappointments, frustrations and mutual support have paid off over time. As one therapist once commented, marriage, in its best form, is a "people making machine," a process that can help us reach our potential if we are willing to do the work that comes with it.

In Thornton Wilder's "The Skin of Our Teeth," Mr. Antrobus says,

> I married you because you gave me a promise. That promise made up for your faults. And the promise I gave you made up for mine. Two imperfect people got married and it was the promise that made the marriage. . . . And when our children were growing up, it wasn't a house that protected them; and it wasn't our love that protected them—it was that promise.[4]

That's what marital faithfulness looks like. It's a promise made and kept by two imperfect people—people with flaws, faults, character weaknesses.

Real commitment isn't based on any feelings or scenarios. It's founded on the vows we made before God and others. It's a pledge we carry out to completion, running over any roadblocks that obstruct us. Marriage is meant to be a total giving of oneself to another. And there's no true fulfillment without risk.

I've compared commitment in marriage to bungee jumping. In that activity, once you take the plunge, there's no turning back and no changing your mind; you're committed to following through.

Commitment means relinquishing the childish dream of having a spouse who gratifies all your needs and desires and who makes up for all childhood disappointments. It means expecting and accepting that your spouse will disappoint you and at times not live up to your expectations. It means sticking with him or her when difficulties arrive (eventually they will).

A person of commitment knows that marriage is not a prison but a source of freedom *and* security. For that reason, the person of commitment looks to himself first and asks, "How am I contributing to the problem?" People of commitment know they can control only their own thoughts and behavior.[5]

Two things that can lead to commitment's erosion are overestimation and underestimation. For example, it's easy to underestimate the level of satisfaction in a marriage while at the same time overestimating the number of problems. A distorted view of what's actually going on in a couple's relationship—as seen by one or both partners—usually happens because they're like mules wearing blinders. Blinders keep the mule from seeing what's going on peripherally. He can see directly ahead, but nothing else.

We frequently get focused on what we think we lack while not seeing all the good all around us. In contrast, focusing on what's working, rather than only obsessing over what isn't, truly does make a difference.

Toward the Marriage You Want

Let's consider your marriage at the present time. Right now. *Today.*

Maybe the marriage you're bringing into your later years has the foundation you want for building an even stronger relationship. Or perhaps you currently find it unsatisfying, lacking some or many of the elements needed for building. While there are many variations of "marriage models" to consider, I've selected the following one, which includes the following "styles," because so many say they can relate to it.[6]

The Devitalized Marriage

Self-explanatory, this placid, half-alive relationship is missing emotional involvement, conflict, and passion. Both individuals can be thought of as "married singles," living as separately as possible but remaining "together."

This sort of married life could be described as an exchange of services. It could be that the husband provides money for running the household and leaves the details to the wife. He's consumed with work and hobbies, and interaction concerning the children or the home happens only when absolutely necessary. Communication is at surface level; there's no sharing of thoughts or feelings. Sex is routine and obligatory (if it even exists).

What do you think will happen at the empty-nest stage and beyond?

The Constant-Conflict Marriage

This style refers to a couple that fights constantly, though amazingly they seem to enjoy it and can't seem to live without it. Over the years they've developed skill and finesse in striking, slashing, and stabbing. At some point they find themselves in a dilemma: They realize their methods are essentially destructive, but they feel unable to change.

Sometimes the comfort they experience in being hostile and hurtful is founded in how, consequently, they blame each other for their unhappiness. The aggression, through straightforward outbursts and/or subtle undercutting, consistently inflicts fresh wounds before the previous ones have had time to develop protective scabs. Both seem to thrive on the volatility, and while their involvement level is intense, it's damaging and painful.

What do you think will happen at the empty-nest stage and beyond?

The Passive-Congenial Marriage

This comfortable (comfort-based?) relationship has few ups and downs. Somewhat similar to the "devitalized marriage" but with slightly more involvement, the involvement isn't dynamic or intensive, and once certain routines have been established they vary little. The humdrum that sets in can last for many years.

What do you think will happen at the empty-nest stage and beyond?

The Total Marriage

This union, characterized by constant togetherness and mutual interest, can be perceived as ideal because "they're so close—they do everything together!" All life experience is shared; little or nothing is done separately.

Their connection is ultra-intense and ultimately fragile: a change or alternation can rock the boat. Since the relationship is everything, individual growth is limited by some degree of smothering and stifling. In time, one or the other may feel bound up and boxed in as his or her efforts to change meet an onslaught of resistance.

Even when suggested adaptations or adjustments are positive and beneficial, the endeavors are blocked. Any deviation upsets the delicate equilibrium that was established and now is cherished. Another title for this is the "eggshell marriage," because one false step and *crunch* goes everything.

What do you think will happen at the empty-nest stage and beyond?

The Vital Marriage

Finally, in the vital marriage, each is highly involved in the other's interests, but they're not into "total" restriction. The couple likes to do things together whenever possible and as much as possible; at the same time, each has maintained individuality and uniqueness. They share roles, and they aren't locked into typical or traditional stereotypes. They openly exchange thoughts and feelings; they prize integrity; their communication is extensive.

> Because marriage is a relationship of shared intimacy, it requires a level of honesty between the partners that goes much deeper than conventional social relationships. People cannot truly share life without knowing each other, and they cannot know each other unless their thoughts are open to each other to a degree that happens in few other human relationships. To be secretive or reserved or defensive toward each other in marriage is inevitably to condemn the relationship to superficiality.[7]

They cooperate in running the home, rearing the children, managing finances, and making decisions. They face and work through disagreements; they're supportive of each other. This marriage usually contains reasonably well-adjusted people willing to take the risk of making changes to enhance and enrich their relationship.

What do you think will happen at the empty-nest stage and beyond?

Take a look at the progression of your marital relationship. Thinking back on the five "types" above, remember that some elements of each (or more than one, or several) may be seen in your marriage. Those categories are not rigid; they often overlap.

1. On the graph below, circle the point opposite the "marriage type" that best describes your marital relationship during each year of your marriage. Then connect the circles in chronological order and trace your marital pattern across, from left to right. You may find an upward curve, indicating improvement. You may find a downward slope, indicating deterioration. Or you may find that your connected points form an up-and-down line or one that remains somewhat level.

Marriage Type	Years Married													
	1	2	4	6	8	10	12	14	16	18	20	22	24	26
Vital														
Total														
Passive-Congenial														
Constant-Conflict														
Devitalized														

2. What did you do to cause your marriage to improve or deteriorate?

3. What did your spouse do to cause improvement or deterioration?

4. If your marriage has been or is in any of the first four categories, what did you do to bring the marriage there or keep it there?

5. What did your spouse do to bring your marriage there or keep it there?

6. You will need goals and a plan in order to achieve change and growth. Looking at your marriage presently, what do you feel needs to be done to move it forward? What will be your goals? Your plan?

7. List specific attitudes and behaviors on your part and on your spouse's. For example: "Perform a new kind act toward him/her"; "Give at least one compliment each day"; "Mentally list his/her positive points."

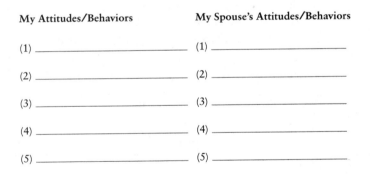

My Attitudes/Behaviors	My Spouse's Attitudes/Behaviors
(1) _____	(1) _____
(2) _____	(2) _____
(3) _____	(3) _____
(4) _____	(4) _____
(5) _____	(5) _____

Don't Guilt, Don't Grab . . . Give Grace

What can we do to give our marriage the opportunity to be all we've wanted it to be at this stage? After fifty years of marriage as well as teaching on this subject and counseling hundreds of couples, I've discussed a few principles that make a difference. Here are a few ideas.

As Christians we're called to give our spouse the benefit of the doubt, to cut him or her some slack—that is, we're to extend grace.

You can start doing this by simply refusing to assume the worst when your spouse does something out of the ordinary. When that happens, don't assume he or she has ulterior motives or is angry or upset with you. Instead, start with the assumption of good intentions.

One day I was bass fishing over some sunken trees. While retrieving my lure after a cast, a large bass took it and proceeded to strip the line from my reel. I did my best to turn the fish before it plowed deeper into the trees, but he managed to wrap himself and the line around a trunk.

I saw him for just a second before he went deep, and I knew he was a big one. I wanted to land him, and I had a couple options. First, I could engage in a tug-of-war, pulling harder on the line to try pulling him out from the stump. This seemed like the obvious choice: initiate a power struggle and show who's in charge. But I knew this would backfire; the line would rub against the wood until it frayed and broke. I'd lose both the fish and the lure in his mouth.

Or, second, I could take the pressure off, *cut some slack* in the line, and let the fish have freedom to move around on his own. Then perhaps he'd unwrap himself and swim away from the stump. This meant giving up some control and letting him do as he wished for a while. It was going to take patience. If this were to work, it would be on his terms and in his own time.

I cut him slack, and then I waited. Slowly, the line began to move, and when he swam out from the stump I was ready. After a brief struggle, I landed him, took a picture, and released him to grow even larger.

I realized the way I'd handled that fish resembles how many of us need to learn to handle our spouses. Just as that bass came my way when he was cut some slack, so our spouses often do the same when we don't rely on power grabs, suffocation, passive-aggression, or guilt trips. Couples who give up trying to confine and control each other and instead give grace discover higher satisfaction in marriage.

No matter how long you've been together, the fact that you're together means you've developed coping and adjustment (C&A) skills. You've made it to this place in your life, and that's no accident. Every couple goes through difficult times; some grow through the process, while others watch their marriage erode.

Keeping this in mind, take the opportunity to make your own C&A marital-history timeline. A little below the top of a blank page, draw a horizontal line, and write your wedding date on the extreme left. Below this line, from left to right, list significant events with their year of occurrence, then indicate with a letter *P* or *N* whether it was more of a positive or negative experience. Above the line, very briefly, note how you coped and adjusted.

Now, beneath this timeline, write a paragraph for each item, explaining in more detail how you coped and adjusted; write also about what you learned. Doing this may encourage you as you realize what you've accomplished and are capable of doing. Further, it could be useful in regard to the adjustments you'll need to make in your life's future stages.

The Staying Power of Praying Together

Many couples at all stages struggle with how to pray together. In counseling and in seminars, I often suggest that they start by praying *for* each other. Give serious thought to this. Try praying for your spouse daily, whenever he or she comes to mind, asking for God's guidance and blessing.

Some take another step and begin calling or messaging each other to say they're praying and to ask what they can pray about. Others, as they prepare to part in the morning, ask, "How can I best pray for you today?"

How important is this? One husband said,

> Without a relationship with God, I don't see how we would have made it through some rough times. Before we got married, I believed very strongly that my future wife knew God also. This was key to me, because when the impasses came, I knew the same Spirit that was at work in me was at work in her. If I would respond positively to God, and she would also, I knew we would make it. Many times the only thing I could do to keep from self-destruction or blasting her away was to pray. I would either get away by myself or invite her to join me as I led in prayer. I believe the focus on God and mutual faith has pulled us to Him and to each other. It's fair to say, I don't know where I'd be without God!

Perhaps shared prayer is already part of your life. If it isn't, this may be what breathes new life into your marriage. This is a choice you can make to take a positive step.

Your decisions and your actions thereafter are what build the memories, feelings, and attitudes you'll carry through your later years. Some couples will have fewer memories, whereas others will have a deep reservoir of savored experiences, but no matter your age or the length of your marriage, there's still time to make a choice. You *can* enhance your marriage; you *can* make it even more fulfilling.

At a marriage seminar a few years ago, one couple stood and shared with us the goals they'd selected for their marriage. I vividly remember one of them: "When we reach our fiftieth anniversary, we will be able to look back and say the last ten years have been the best." Believe it: A goal like this is within reach!

Some might picture the latter years of marriage as the overcast, dismal close of a long and tiring day. They needn't be. Those years could reflect all the radiant brilliance of a jaw-dropping sunset, one that heralds an even better coming day. A day of discovery, of praise, of joy, of belonging, of love. A sunset that looks very much like a sunrise.

Recommended Reading

The Five Love Languages, Gary Chapman, Northfield

Love & Respect, Emerson Eggerichs, Thomas Nelson

Communication: Key to Your Marriage, H. Norman Wright, Regal

Quiet Times for Couples, H. Norman Wright, Harvest House

His Needs, Her Needs, Willard F. Harley, Revell

7

The Boomerang Generation

There's an event occurring more frequently in family life today, one that can change not just one family but several. The results seem to linger indefinitely, even unendingly. Whether it's your child or someone else's (e.g., your in-laws) in this situation, it can markedly alter your life and theirs.

An adult child who divorces often returns home.

The realization that this is happening can be especially shocking and upsetting for the parents. It's also disruptive for their present and future plans.

Just as when your children marry you can feel that imaginary connective string stretching out, so when they divorce you can feel it rolling back up. The family expands and contracts with every addition or subtraction of a member. When divorce strikes your family through your child, the alliances and divisions throughout the entire extended family shift, and some even break.

When divorce occurs, you experience many pushes and pulls on near and dear relationships. In this sense it's useful to think of your family as a mobile. Cutting the string between any two parts unbalances the whole structure until it's repaired. Your whole family reverberates when your child divorces; the mobile goes on a tilt.[1]

Your own marriage can be affected by the different ways each of you handles pain and grief. You may have divergent ideas about how to respond to your son or daughter, to your daughter- or son-in-law, to your ex-in-laws. This is complicated and stressful, especially in this stage of your life.

You may feel that your child's divorce threatens your whole value system. If you're utterly opposed to divorce, regardless of the reason, you'll certainly face difficulty because your convictions have been violated. You may have a hard time explaining it to or discussing it with others; you may feel guilt if you think you failed to pass along your values to your kids.

It's possible you'll discover that the marriage's breakup is due to your son's or daughter's unfaithfulness. In the fallout, some parents have had to deal with all matter of collateral damage; sometimes even sexually transmitted diseases. Some find out the marriage failed because their own child abused his spouse.

Any parents in such a scenario should be prepared for an onslaught of anger once the situational shock hits and begins to dissipate. They may find themselves brooding over the circumstances for many weeks or months. While doing the dishes or driving alone they may fuss and stew about "how easily those two gave up on their commitment." In the face of such disruption you might feel anger at what caused it, who caused it, and how all this is affecting everyone involved. These emotions (and others) are normal.

Unanswerable questions arise: "Why didn't they try harder or longer to work it out? How could they not have gone for help? Why didn't they see this coming? Can they really just throw it all away? Where's the effort, the patience, the endurance that every marriage takes?" Parents want to be supportive, yet a part of them disagrees strongly with what's happening. They begin to worry; they agonize over how this will affect their child's job, self-esteem, financial future. (They might even worry about their own.)

You'll begin to anticipate the possible losses caused by this divorce. Gatherings, visits, birthdays, and holidays will change. You won't be viewing the wedding videos or photos so often. The upcoming extended family vacation . . . it'll be different, or it might not even happen.

Your anger may be accompanied by a need to blame, and you'll have a number of targets for venting. In-laws . . . the attorney . . . friends who had a negative influence . . . maybe even your own spouse for what he or she did or didn't do, things you think somehow contributed to the problems.

You may drop some blame on yourself. Maybe you'll start taking stock of what you did or didn't do, doubting your adequacy, retroactively weighing your suggestions and sifting your words. If you've largely stayed out of issues or conflicts, you may feel you should've been more available, offered more advice, just . . . *been there*, spatially and/or spiritually. Could you have helped more with expenses? . . . Should you have volunteered to babysit more so they'd have had opportunities to be and bond together? . . . Or perhaps you think you helped too *much*, to the point of interfering or enabling.

Be sure that you don't try to avoid your emotions or pretend you aren't having certain feelings. Instead of shutting down or exploding, seek to "let them out" without attacking or bombarding others. One helpful approach is to write some uncensored letters—for yourself, but in the voice you'd need to use if you were addressing one specific person or another.

If it isn't something that he or she actually needs to hear from you, write out the feelings and thoughts as if you were speaking them. Reading them aloud to yourself may assist you in releasing the emotions.

Guidance for Grandparents

If you have grandchildren, much of your pain will center around their hurt and struggle as they try to work through their parents' breakup.

If your adult child is a noncustodial parent, you'll end up hurting more, and you'll likely feel powerless if you find it more difficult to spend time with your grandkids. If your son or daughter retains custody, you will need to guard against falling into the trap of doing too much for the grandchildren as a means of seeking to compensate for your pain and sadness. However, in a study of freshmen at two major universities, 96 percent said their grandparents were "extremely important" or "important" in their lives; 90 percent said they wish they could have spent more time with their grandparents than they did.

All states have visitation laws for grandparents. You'll be able to visit your grandkids as long as you're able to show it's in their best interest. What exactly is their best interest? How can you as a grandparent best help them?

They'll need lots of love and acceptance. They tend to have confidence in what gives them stability. Grandparents are their connection with the past.

At first being around them may feel like walking on eggshells. It's typical to struggle with what to say, and you don't know what they might ask. The best you can do is to be available and to listen. Let your grandchildren initiate the discussion, and check with your adult child to see what they've been told and what the parents would like to have said.

Some grandparents end up resenting other grandparents. And some have had to go to court just to ensure their own visitation rights. But if your child had children in the marriage, it's more than likely you always will have some contact and interaction with the other set of grandparents.

After such a divorce, in addition to self-concerns, any grandparent needs to deal also with those of the grandkids. Will there be enough money to care for them well? Will they come home from school to an empty house? What if the custodial parent has his or her new romantic interest stay overnight, or even move in? How will the divorce affect the self-esteem and academic performance? How will their birthdays, games, and trips be handled?

They may raise their own concerns and questions, either directly or through their behavior. If you're that grandparent, here are some common concerns and some responses you can give:

1. *"Who will take care of me?"* Pledge that you can, at intervals or for a period of time. Adolescents need a kind of babysitting too.

2. *"Is anything in the world reliable and predictable?"* Make a special effort to be there for them as promised, every time, barring an emergency. When you say you'll pick them up or meet them, arrive on time. Your reliability is crucial.

3. *"Are my parents crazy?"* When the opportune moment arises, explain what an unsettling period this is for both parents. Tell them that, after a while, they and the children will settle down more and more.

4. *"Where is my father/mother now living?"* Encourage visits to the absent parent's home (if that meets with

the custody arrangements). The kids want to feel part of the new setting.

5. *"Will my mother/father—my custodial parent—get sick, have an accident, die?"* You can't promise this won't happen, but let them know you're a backup and so are the cousins, uncles, and aunts from both sides of the family.

6. *"Will we have enough money now?"* Reassure that they will be taken care of. You can help with money or gifts, giving them a weekly allowance or money for a class trip.

7. *"Will I have to change schools now?"* Many children remain where they are and attend the same school. If change is necessary, though, research the new school's positives, visit the classroom if you can, and give much encouragement to the kids.

8. *"Will I have to move to a new neighborhood?"* Recount stories of when you moved: your new room, new friends, the yard. If the move is nearby, remind them that their old friends can visit and stay overnight.

9. *Is Mom going to marry Bob? Will they keep me with them?* You probably can't do much about this one except to wonder with them.[2]

Perhaps one of the most awkward dilemmas is how to relate to your ex-in-laws. Terri, mother of a newly divorced son, said, "Fred wanted me to cut off all contact with his wife's relatives, as he'd done. But I told him, 'You may have divorced your wife, but I'm not divorcing her mother, Ethyl. We've developed a wonderful friendship and prayer partnership over the past fifteen years, and we've both said it will continue. You'll have to learn to accept it.'"

You might always be closer to your child's first set of in-laws than the next set. If you are, and that's your choice, nothing is wrong with it. Or maybe you never did relate well to the in-laws and this isn't a major loss for you, but nevertheless you were especially close to your son-in-law (or daughter-in-law). Even if he destroyed the marriage, you may find it difficult to dislike him—it could be that he was the son (or daughter) you never had. You might feel a push/pull tension and anguish over *why* this had to happen.

It's also not uncommon for a divorcing adult child to move back home for financial reasons. This boomerang variation likewise requires adjustments on the part of all concerned.

> When divorced adult children live in the house belonging to their parents, they naturally feel impotent, unable to cope. They feel as if they're not adult; they have failed. As parents of divorced children, we can repeat, "This is working out all right; it isn't a problem; you're not in the way." But still, grown children who are forced to take charity from their own parents feel demeaned and will often react in bizarre and unpredictable ways. Their loss of self-esteem may cause them to engage in withdrawal, in acts of self-denigration, or sometimes even in hostility. They may lash out in anger against the situation, not realizing that they have picked the wrong target. We always hurt the ones we love because they are close to us.[3]

Regarding adjustments for grandparents, perhaps the new arrangement will affect the proposed sale of your home, which used to be too large. It will change your retirement plans. Possibly it will revise your everyday schedule. It will even impact your intimacy. There's nothing easy about the situation.

> Grandparents can be caught in the middle trying to do the right thing, to be loving and charitable. We often may need to spend a good deal of time in prayer, coming to terms with

understanding our divorced children, forgiving them their outbursts and irresponsible behavior. We must realize that there is a much larger principle at stake here and attempt to provide an environment in which our grandchildren can grow into normalcy and somehow escape the ravages that divorce breeds.[4]

Another major element that can complicate things, which may also prolong the period of adjustment to a divorce, is money.

Your child may need or want to borrow from you during a separation.

You may be approaching retirement and find yourself pulled between saving for yourself and helping your daughter with bills after she's awarded custody of the children.

You may be upset over your child's irresponsible financial behavior and decide to assist your daughter-in-law or son-in-law and the grandchildren.

You may have remorse about having given some family heirlooms to the ex, never dreaming there would be a divorce and that she would keep them.

Maybe you gave the couple a down payment as a wedding gift, but now the house is the ex's.

These and other financial issues may pertain to past gifts and loans. And you can do little about many of them. You can, however, plan for the future. Parents of a divorced child ask questions like these:

How can I be sure my child's ex doesn't get any of his/her inheritance?

How can I ensure he/she doesn't misuse funds I've set aside for the grandchildren?

How can I nullify business arrangements with the ex and his/her family?

Your child needs assistance from an attorney, and, in these cases and others, maybe you will also.

As for in-laws, in time, a redesigned semblance of stability may be upset again when you learn your family tree is about to have unfamiliar branches grafted onto it. For instance, your child says she's getting married again . . . to someone with three children. You'll be an instant step-grandparent. It's out of your control; you have no choice in the matter.

If you do resist, avoid the following situations/actions:

- *The new spouse is not welcomed in her new in-laws' home (at best, she's coolly tolerated).* I've seen situations where the marriage isn't even recognized. In one, the wife was referred to as "that woman and her children." Some grandparents sabotage the marriage through rejection, manipulation, or rumors. This is the result of classic, unhealthy denial.

- *The new spouse is accepted, but the step-grandparents can't bring themselves to become involved with the new step-grandchildren.* This can cause fewer problems if the children are adolescents or older, but it can be hurtful and damaging in any case.

- *Unequal/unfair treatment of grandchildren vs. step-grandchildren.* This is a difficult scenario because the grandparents' feelings for their original grandkids are usually positive, and it's natural for them to feel that the others have been thrust upon them.

This issue must be discussed with your child and his/her new spouse to clarify expectations and intentions. You'll need to work out creative solutions and will find no perfect answer. Younger kids have difficulty understanding preferential treatment. Older ones can learn to understand that grandparents will do more for grandchildren they've known from birth, as long as the differences don't blatantly emphasize feelings of being discounted and rejected.

You might ask the new in-laws how they would like you to relate to their children; share your own concerns and struggles. One stepmom was relieved to discover that her new daughter-in-law didn't expect her to take her children to the lake each summer (as she did her own grandkids) and didn't want her to feel obligated.

- *A grandchild is born to this new marriage.* The grandparents may tend to favor the new child because he/she is part of their family line. This will be obvious to the step-grandchildren.

Feelings cannot be forced to develop. However, you may be surprised to find blessings in the new relationships as time goes on. The new children may never have had grandparents, and you could end up filling some unmet needs. You may enjoy a relationship with the new grandchildren or the new spouse that you never expected.

Neither side should force itself upon the other. Give it time. Learn how to pray specifically for the new family members. If they haven't been involved in church or aren't believers, they can become part of your mission field.

Planning to Be Practical

Any adult child returning to his parents' home for any reason can disrupt plans and dreams. Though they also can be a blessing, you and your boomerang child are in for role changes. You can't go back to the way you were; neither can they. So establish guidelines and evaluate both parties' expectations. If each would make a list of these and then discuss them, you'll eliminate many conflicts in advance. Talk about how each expects to be treated.

Practically, it may be helpful to relate to him or her as a boarder. Create and discuss guidelines; sign a "contract" and post it somewhere as a reminder. Clarify the basics, like chores—who does what and for whom? In terms of privacy, who uses which rooms? When, and for what purpose? What about meals—who buys, cooks, cleans up, and when?

What's the possible or actual length of stay? Financial arrangements—who pays for what? Food, rent, utilities, auto repairs, cleaning, and other expenses or factors come to the forefront.

In various ways, the younger generations have different values and morals than the ones we were raised with and/ or have embraced. Parents are shocked and frustrated over choice of dress, friends, lifestyle, sexual choices or preference, attitudes, education, and vocation, and not just during the adolescent years. This can happen when the now-adult child is in his twenties, thirties, or even forties or older.

When it's abuse of alcohol and other drugs that has caused a marriage to self-destruct, it's natural for parents not only to be emotionally stunned but also to try to help. They've invested many years and tears up to now, and they can become desperate to see him turn things back around. However, parents are sometimes the last people an adult child will listen to. Be sure that you don't create or get drawn into a codependent relationship. If you need professional counseling or pastoral help, take the needed steps to get it.

8

The Gathering of Losses

Our culture is one of gathering. We especially like to accumulate things. Meeting that challenge is a reflection upon our abilities and our station. There's no limit to what some will do in the quest for stuff.

But there's one exception. We don't like to accumulate losses. We often go to great lengths to avoid them. We'll even deny they're a part of life.

As I said earlier, loss is necessary. During life's first half, losses are part of growth and development. Some are actually celebrated as well as mourned, since many are developmental.

In the second part of life, losses become more frequent, more permanent, and usually more negative. They take on a different feel, a different character. They tend to build upon one another, linked together, adding up ominously.

Your life and mine are made up of attachments. When these dissolve or break, we move into the world of grief. The more we're vested in something, whether a person or a role, the more we grieve when it's taken away.

The losses we experience in life's second half are fairly predictable. These, in one way or another, include family, marriage, health, work, status, and friends. Each loss has a meaning to it that impacts us.

It's important to understand the uniqueness of loss and grief in our later years. This will keep us from being blindsided and prepare us to handle them.

First of all, losses will occur faster. You may have lost an acquaintance or friend to death when you were younger, but as we age this tends to become a more regular occurrence. We find ourselves scanning the obituaries more frequently. It's a fact: With time's passage, losses through death will increase.

What about health? Limitations begin to be a standard part of living. Every part of our body seems subject to attack—from vision to hearing to digestion, from ligaments to bones to all the various replacements. (Guess what also tends to become the focus of our conversations!)

Further, it's not just one loss we'll have difficulty handling. Multiple, repeated events will complicate both our grieving and our adjustment. Thus you might find it helpful to complete a loss history, from birth to the present time. You could be surprised at the number of losses you've experienced and at their escalation in recent years. Again, the more we learn about loss and grief in advance, the better we are at coping and growing.

Another characteristic of loss during this phase is finality. Losing a spouse or a job while older doesn't give you much of an opportunity window for finding a new one. As one man said, there can be a sense of a door slamming shut and staying locked. Another said that as we get older we truly must become friends with loss and grief. As we age we'll probably grieve several losses at once, and some won't be fully resolved while on earth.

One characteristic of loss during this time, though, is that most losses can be anticipated. Think about your life five to ten years from now. You may not want to, but it's necessary. You'll need to prepare for the possibility that you could lose your spouse, or an adult child, or a job or career, or an aspect of your health, or an ability, or a friend. You might have a change of residence.

Feeling Summed Up by Subtractions

Whenever there's a loss that will be lasting, we need to come to the place of saying good-bye to whom or what it was. Thereby acceptance (rather than resistance) can move in, and then we can move forward to experience life in a new way. Moving forward after loss involves relearning our world, and as we age this could become a constant. Fortunately, we *can* still learn as we age.

The first step in handling a loss is admitting it, perhaps by saying it aloud. Here's one I can say (maybe you can too): "I am no longer young." In fact, I'm not even middle-aged!

I realized this a number of years ago. I really felt it a couple years back when I went back to my favorite place of all time—Grand Teton National Park. I'd been there to vacation and to conduct marriage-enrichment seminars twenty-six times. I'd fished, hiked, and climbed up and down slopes throughout the forest. But it had been thirteen years since my last visit; I was in my late fifties then, and now I'm in my early seventies.

What a difference. Somehow they'd made the slopes steeper, the paths thicker with brush and logs . . . they'd even thinned the air. This experience prompted me to go to a gym and hire a trainer, which helped tremendously. When I returned to the Tetons again a year later, I had a better experience.

Your body changes in how it works *and* in how it looks. When you see yourself in a photo, you may start feeling a negative response to your size, shape, contour, hair color or thickness. Our body doesn't lie—it tells us what's occurring, and ultimately we're at its mercy.

You will feel grief about body changes. It's okay to say, out loud, "My body is not the same. It doesn't do what it used to do; it doesn't look like it did. I'm learning to accept that, and I commit to being thankful for what I have. It's still a temple of the Holy Spirit, and God can use me and bless me."

You might feel a loss of acceptance or acclaim in your profession. In some occupations being older is valued and rewarded, but in many others the younger minds and abilities are most sought after. You'll need to keep the pain of a sense of rejection from overshadowing the other areas of your life.

There are intangible losses as well, and they can be significant. Some are the losses of dreams. Certain dreams of our youth were attainable; some were perhaps delusional. It could be that we attained some dreams while others fell by the wayside. As we age, we realize that some will never be fulfilled.

Judith Viorst spoke of the life cycle's many "necessary" losses, ones we must endure in order to grow into life's next phase.

> We may start to feel that this is a time of always letting go, of one thing after another after another: our waistlines. Our vigor. Our sense of adventure. Our 20/20 vision. Our trust in justice. Our earnestness. Our playfulness. Our dream of being a tennis star, or a TV star, or a senator. We give up hoping to read all the books we once had vowed to read, and to go to all the places we'd once vowed to visit. We give up hoping we'll save the world from cancer or from war. We even give up hoping that we will succeed in becoming underweight or immortal.[1]

In *Losses in Later Life,* Scott Sullender said:

> Fantasies, dreams and illusions are subtle things to lose. It is
> not like losing a home or a spouse or a damaged leg. These
> are not concrete entities. Nevertheless, they are very real, very
> powerful and very determinative to our well-being. See, most
> of us fashion our identities around our dreams. We build a
> sense of who we are based on our dreams. We plan our life's
> script around the dreams that we feel we are supposed to
> fulfill. And our self-esteem rises or falls with the achievement
> of these dreams. We cannot "live" without dreams. Humans
> are dreamers. This is why the loss of dreams that comes with
> later life can invoke such subtle but powerful feelings.[2]

Family losses occur in many forms, and for a while as we
age it feels as though we're caught in a vise, being squeezed
by losses on either side, kids as well as parents. Once more,
some are predictable, like children becoming independent
and moving out and establishing families, or our own parents
aging and dying. Our children will always be our children
but won't always function or interact as children; they'll become adults and friends. If our desire is to relive our lives
in them, we'll probably face more disappointment than we
anticipated. Of our dreams and expectations for our kids,
many won't be met.

We never planned for our daughter to take a detour. Then,
for four years, we felt we were in an emotional Death Valley. It
was the second-most difficult time in our parenting role (after
when, two years earlier, we placed Matthew in a home for the
disabled). From one crisis to another, we faced situations we'd
heard of in other families but had never planned to encounter.

Who would have thought Sheryl's fiancé would turn out
to be a drug dealer and a physical abuser? Or that she would
have to move home because of an untenably difficult situation
with a roommate?

Say an adult child drops a bomb—leaves his spouse for another, is arrested for embezzlement, falls into alcoholism. You were able to guide your child through the perils of adolescence, and now you've let down your guard. But then the news hits. It's a crisis and a loss. And you're dealing with your own developmental losses as well.

If you were dependent on your adult child in any way, you may feel torn between her newfound need to be dependent on you and your own needs and wants. You may be called on to help in a way that could tax your resources or cripple your retirement. You might wonder whether it's even okay for you to be having these thoughts and feelings.

The Passing of Parents

In addition, the death of a parent at any time is a major loss to any child. It changes your life in so many ways; it brings the loss of certain hopes and dreams. It can be the death of part of your past as well as part of your present and future. If your past with your parents was lacking, regardless of their age, you may have been looking forward to a new future with them, and now that's gone. Perhaps you had questions to ask, grievances to share, a confrontation you'd waited years to express. That opportunity is lost along with them.

As your identity undergoes change, in a way you feel abandoned. Your sense of loss is affected by their spiritual condition as well. You'll miss your parents no matter what. Do you know or wonder whether they were believers?

These are the most commonly expressed statements when a parent dies:

- I feel like an orphan.
- Now I'm closer to death.
- I feel vulnerable.

114

- I'm frustrated—there was something more I needed to say or do.
- I am released from a burden.[3]

These reactions come about because most of us never think a parent's death is actually going to occur. Yes, we know it will, but a part of us denies it. When a parent dies, you feel the protection of your own life dissolve. One man in his fifties said, "When my mom died, I felt like my home had been taken away. I was cut adrift."

At least four factors affect the way you may react to the loss. It helps to ask yourself the following questions:

1. *How did my parent die?* A sudden, unexpected loss will be more of a shock than a gradual one, although the pain is the same.

2. *What was the quality of the relationship with my parent?* Was there any unfinished business?

3. *What's the amount of support I received during the grief process?* If they're still living, what support will you have when the time comes?

4. *How will my past experiences with loss affect this loss?*[4]

Sometimes the death brings a sense of relief and a feeling of safety never before experienced. For example, if a parent was a bully or an abuser, you can feel relief along with your grief. Some of that grief is over the relationship you never had. Many still long for the parent they would've loved to have loved.[5]

If there have been months (or more) of suffering, death can be a release and relief. The process isn't always clear-cut, though. Some feel that they stop and start their grief repeatedly, depending on their parents' daily health.

For many, a parent's death feels like the beginning of your own: "If my dad could die, then so can I." Death of parents is the most common form of bereavement for adults. Depending on the relationship, again, response can range from ambivalence to deep sorrow. One primary factor influencing grief, however, is the parent's age and yours. There's a major difference between losing a parent in your twenties versus your fifties or sixties.

> The fact that you weren't there when he died can also be a source of long-lasting regret. The fact that *no one* may have been there can also be stressful. You may have to deal with the lengthy, painful mental process of second-guessing. *If only* your parent had taken a later train, *if only* they had consulted a doctor earlier and so on. Sudden deaths are often bizarre, like nightmares, because they are so unexpected.[6]

Consider the following:

- What if your parent was living life to the fullest? That makes death even more untimely. If your parent was senile or just waiting to go home to Jesus, some feelings are of relief, i.e., "It was a blessing."

- Is this the first or second parent to die, and how many deaths have you experienced before? If it's the first, not only can the shock be intense, but also you'll have concern for the remaining parent.

- When both parents die, there's no longer a generation between you and death. The buffer's gone; *you're* the older generation. Explore your thoughts and feelings so you can accept this new position.

Some of the potential adjustments for you with this loss are:

- Your chances are lost to resolve past unpleasantness.

- You can no longer help your parent in a way you wanted. Maybe you're now in a position to return favors, but it can't be done.

- If you've never separated emotionally from your parents and couldn't make decisions without their approval, now what?

Anyone who loses a parent may try to stay connected in some way. The activities vary but might include the following:

- Imagining the parent in some distant place; seeking to make sense of their experience.

- Experiencing the deceased parents by believing they are watching or communicating, perhaps through dreams.

- Reaching out to the deceased parent by visiting the cemetery and/or talking to them. Waking memories—e.g., thinking about them in literal terms—are very common.

- "Linking" objects, such as carrying around something the deceased owned. This tends to keep the adult child living in the past but also symbolically can become a transitional object.[7]

Another common death-of-a-parent result is change in relationships with siblings. The event can serve to help build *or* destroy them. Some people feel the burden's on them, especially if there'd been internal fighting to protect a given family member. One great source of inter-sibling conflict is the will and estate. Estrangement often occurs with parental death and the aftermath.[8]

When a parent is terminally ill, you may see a personality change. This can be from pain, medication, or awareness of impending death. You may also see an absence of personality, especially if there's dementia or Alzheimer's.[9]

Your role has changed dramatically. You may be looked at as the senior advisor in your family system. Now is a time to look at your parents' last years and ask yourself, "Is this how I want to spend the last years of my life? If not, what changes do I need to make?"

Ask, "What do I want to model and leave for those coming behind me?" Along with the empty space in your life, there's a new opportunity to create and influence. Scott Sullender put it well:

> This new life stage can be the most productive and creative of our life cycle. But it will be so only if we are able to say "good-bye" to our parents and not cling to them. The living God bids us to grieve. For only in grief will we again find new life.[10]

Beyond Family

One oft-overlooked loss is the death of a friend. After it happens, in the subsequent weeks you'll find yourself reaching for the phone to call her, to share something you had in common, to set up a time to get together . . . but only a dial tone's at the other end.

Friends take an investment of time and understanding. Some are closer than some family members; some fill roles from confidante to sounding board to sports companion to mentor. I have seven close ones, currently ranging in age from sixty-two to seventy-five. At times I wonder which of us will reach the banquet table first.

Each has been in my life thirty to forty years, and we've shared much together. The death of friends like these leaves a permanent hole—there isn't time or opportunity or energy to build a new relationship. What happens when such a friend dies? Probably not much, or at least not enough. Cards, calls, and condolences likely will be lacking, since it wasn't a family member but "just a friend." For you, though, it's inexpressibly significant, especially now in a high-tech world where it's more difficult to build these bonds.

Then there's loss of a vocation. Your response when someone asks what you do is, "Well, I used to . . ." We've addressed retirement issues elsewhere, but, briefly, being eased out of a job or demoted can bring an abundance of losses, and again, you need to indentify and address each secondary loss created from the loss of work. Those who adjust will redirect their abilities and energies elsewhere and often discover more fulfillment now than when they were receiving the paycheck. When we work as an expression of our relationship with Jesus Christ, our life consistently sees renewal.[11]

In response to "What loss do you feel is still unresolved?" one man said:

> As far as I know, I am working with the grief that I'm aware of. My progress in processing varies, as does the felt level of the grief over time. If loss is resolved when grief is no longer felt, then I guess some loss may be lingering because I still feel a sense of grief related to my father, mother, job once in a while and even the loss of my younger self on rare occasions. It is possible there may be losses I haven't identified yet or decided to release, such as my sister who has cut herself off from the rest of our family and doesn't wish to be contacted by us. I wrote a letter to her, saying what I needed to say, nearly eight years ago and then let go of my expectations when it wasn't answered.
>
> The ultimate loss is still waiting for me but I don't think about it much except in terms of what experiences I'd still like to participate in while I am still able.

Once in a while I think of the experiences of my children and grandchildren that I won't be around to witness after I'm gone and feel a bit of sadness.

No matter what you're experiencing or have yet to experience, consider these words:

We should not "borrow from the future" by living in fear of the next life stage. Neither should we live in the past by "idolizing" the life stage just completed. Live fully in the present. Enjoy it. Embrace it. Look for God there. However, in order to fully embrace the present, we must regularly let go of the past, and one of the most significant losses that we must periodically let go of is the loss of our youth.[12]

9

You're Older: Rejoice!

Getting old—becoming mature, aging—expressions for the process of growing elderly. What images or terms come to mind when you see these words? For many it's not a positive image, which may indicate why we resist or try to delay but not embrace the process. Some stereotype euphemisms are

a person in poor health

declining mentally

slow and stuck

can't change or doesn't want to

nonproductive

going downhill physically

As we age we'll have to contend with the culture's prominent messages.

Youthfulness is best. Delay or mask the process by eliminating wrinkles, gray hair, white hair, lack of hair, sagging parts, out-of-date clothes and toys.

You needn't age. Just look at the ads for seniors online, on TV, in the papers and magazines. If we bought every pill and device to feel and look young, we'd go broke. Many illustrations depict seniors not "acting their age."

Senior opinions aren't worth much. Out of touch, we need to make room for the younger, smarter generations. Advertisers want the attention of those who will spend money, not those with decreasing or stabilized income.

The older generation is less productive. Some question our value if we're no longer in the work force. It's much more difficult to get a job also, particularly one that utilizes your life-long skills and abilities. "Modern progress lowers the value of older people at the same time as it adds years to our lives. The longer we live the less we are worth, and we *will* live longer!"[1]

We do lose some mental ability. Ambition and energy may diminish. Our bodies change; we can't do what we once did; physical issues can be a major concern. *Dementia! Senility! Alzheimer's!* are words that strike fear into our hearts, too, for it seems we can better handle the body's deterioration than the mind's. One in four over the age of eighty is impacted by dementia.

Becoming Expectant About "Life Expectancy"

However, look at the large numbers *not* afflicted. Our minds may operate more slowly, and short-term memory may not be as sharp, but most aspects of intelligence and memory stay intact. We can change directions, and we can adjust to slowing down and to disease.

What we do to stretch and exercise our brain impacts what happens. Creativity doesn't necessarily decrease with age. Many do their best work as they get older, and why not? All the years of experience and accumulated wisdom count for something. The attitude factor can make such a difference.[2]

The Bible offers a positive heritage. Old age is a blessing, a gift from God to be valued by the whole community. Old Testament law commanded all to rise in the presence of the aged.[3] When Job's theologian friends sat down with him to debate God's justice, their conversation assumed that elders normally had the edge in sorting out difficult questions.[4] We're to respect people who have aged. The commandment to honor parents[5] is a specific application of the wider expectation that you honor your elders.

Isaac, Jacob, Eli, and Ahijah all suffered from failing eyesight. Barzillai was hard of hearing and lost his sense of taste. David developed chronically poor circulation.[6] As Scripture demonstrates, old age isn't ideal.

The author of Ecclesiastes gave a graphic view of aging:

> Remember your Creator
> in the days of your youth,
> before the days of trouble come
> and the years approach when you will say,
> "I find no pleasure in them"—
> before the sun and the light
> and the moon and the stars grow dark,
> and the clouds return after the rain;
> when the keepers of the house tremble [hands],
> and the strong men stoop [legs],
> when the grinders cease because they are few [teeth],
> and those looking through the windows grow dim
> [eyes],
> when the doors to the street are closed [isolation]
> and the sound of grinding fades [loss of strength,
> work];

> when people rise up at the sound of birds [insomnia],
>   but all their songs grow faint [hearing];
> when people are afraid of heights
>   and of dangers in the streets [fear];
> when the almond tree blossoms [white hair]
>   and the grasshopper drags itself along [ungainly
>   walk]
>   and desire no longer is stirred [impotence].
> Then people go to their eternal home
>   and mourners go about the streets [death].[7]

With such a frank perspective, it's a wonder anyone would wish to experience it. Yet for the Old Testament Jew, long life was a prime benefit of godly living.[8] There's no biblical prayer for seeking to avoid its difficulties, no request for remaining young. Conversely, the author of Psalm 71 prays for God's saving presence through the time of trial:

> Do not cast me away when I am old;
>   do not forsake me when my strength is gone. . . .
> Even when I am old and gray,
>   do not forsake me, my God.[9]

Another psalm seems to answer, expressing the assurance of God's care, acquired through decades of experience:

> I was young and now I am old,
>   yet I have never seen the righteous forsaken
>   or their children begging bread.[10]

They loved life; they saw all of it, even the hard parts, as a gift. It came from God's very breath, forming and animating the dust; it required no justification, only thankfulness. The Hebrews feared death but not in a terrified way. It was an end they knew they must one day encounter, yet they had confidence that God could and would sustain them.[11]

As believers, our calling is not to treat aging as a disease to be prevented, or treated and cured. God, the giver of life, doesn't indicate a normative life span or say that following Him and His guidance guarantees longevity. The more important question isn't how long we live but how we live.

That doesn't mean it's wrong to desire a long life. In 1900 middle age was the end! In 1950 it was the door to old age called "Over the Hill," and the only place to go was down. Today it's the gateway to a second adulthood—the second phase of *productive* adulthood.[12]

Our life expectancy has doubled since the nineteenth century. We can either rejoice or despair over this, as the change also has brought something we now refer to as "age-related" diseases that can affect mobility, elimination, vision, or hearing. And we tend to resist the aging process even more.

More than a hundred million Americans use anti-aging products and practices. There's a "120-Year Diet" as well as plastic surgery, human growth hormone, and handfuls of vitamins. For their October 2010 issue, *Good Housekeeping* conducted lab tests on ninety skin products and gave out Anti-Aging Awards. (They added an article on how to "age-proof" your hair.)

Researchers have slowed aging in multi-cell organisms and animals through breeding, genetic manipulation, and dietary alteration. Life-extension organizations identify "longevity genes," which they hope will be useful in creating drugs to slow the aging process and to impact disease.[13] Most of us will experience an extended life, so most of us can expect "gradual dying."

Over the next quarter-century, the number of the elderly will double (to more than seventy million). The fastest-growing group: those over eighty-five, the high-risk group for illness and disability. If you're sixty-five now, one day you probably will need an average of three years long-term care and likely will rely on family members. Thirty-five percent already receive nursing home care. Ten percent of those over sixty-five have Alzheimer's; for those over eighty-five it's more than half.[14]

Taking Stock of Your Real Investments

In addition to life expectancy, we have a productive-, a health-, a family life-, and a financial-expectancy. I'm writing this book at seventy-three and in my mind are other books I'd like to create. However, many midlife individuals I talk with don't have much of a future orientation. Some struggle with this season of the disappointed dreamer: "Is this the time to give up or go on? Can I invent a new dream?"

Did you have a dream? Who was its author? Was it attained?

A company that undergoes an audit can use it to discover where they are with resources, see where they truly stand in profit/loss terms, and determine where to go in the future. In order to move forward, you need to know where you are, so do a personal audit. What's the portrait of your life right now?

Patrick Morley suggested the following audit items:

- Your overall satisfaction
- Milestones
- Major goals, met and unmet
- Significant achievements and satisfying results
- Priorities, right and wrong
- Failures and lessons learned
- Regrets and things you want to improve
- Met and unmet dreams
- Fears, doubts, pressures, concerns about past, present, and future[15]

Consider the terms our culture commonly equates with this phase of life. How do you react when you hear words like *senior citizen* or *golden years*?

ancient	enduring	superannuated
antediluvian	faded	timeworn
antiquated	frail	tough
antique	fusty	used up
archaic	gray	useless
brittle	grizzled	venerable
bygone	hoary	veteran
dated	lasting	vintage
decayed	long-lived	weathered
decrepit	mature	wise
dowdy	passé	withered
dried-up	seasoned	worthless
dry	senile	wrinkled
dusty	shriveled	yellowed[16]
elderly	stale	

Which of these conveys something or anything positive?

We used to define this time by age, by number of years. Increasingly it's defined by a person's state of mental or physical health and amount of physical activity. I've heard us referred to as the "wear and tear" generation.

Likewise, notice new words entering your vocabulary, mostly those that reflect choices to be made about one's future. *Retirement, caregiving, long-term care insurance, advanced directives, hospice,* and *burial planning* are just a few. The older one becomes, the greater the possibility of these words becoming a reality as your losses accumulate.

Have you reached "the *rebounder* stage"?

Rebounder:

1. Someone who springs or bounces back after hitting or colliding with something (in this case, the last stage of life's health problems, struggle to remain independent, and adjustment to the need for care).

2. One who must recover on a repeated basis from depression, health problems, or disappointment.

3. Athlete who retrieves and gains possession of the "ball" as it bounces off the backboard or rim (in this case, one who fights for position to get attention and recognition from adult children, grandchildren or great-grandchildren).

4. One who holds the position of waiting for family members to make the caregiving play as part of the family team.

5. One who lives with the public expectation that one's adult children will make caregiving plans.

6. Rebounders fall into three categories: *Proud Independents,* who struggle to maintain their initial family position and seek to prove their original playing capabilities; *Humble Submissives,* who take a passive role in which they expect to be included in the family game but don't demand to be on the roster; and *Aged Sages,* who strive to maintain their independent position but ask for help when needed and are grateful for the assist.[17]

Which of these most resonates with you? Some say all of the above; others identify two or three with their life at this time. You may want to talk about them with others.

Would you be described as a caring person? As we grow older, hopefully we grow in our capacity and capability to care for others, especially about the generation right behind us. In order to do this, we also must engage in self-care so we don't become an empty shell with nothing left to give. There's a balance, but ideally we move somewhat from self to others. This can be a time when we listen more to our hearts and dreams than ever before.

We need to care for our bodies, which may involve more discipline and exercise than you imagined would be appropriate for those over fifty. The truth is, we've cared mainly about comfort and convenience. Our current lifestyles don't usually provide the physical challenges needed to keep our body at its best; most of us are sedentary, and inactivity overrates activity. We look for elevators without thinking of stairs. We circle endlessly for a vacant spot in the parking lot instead of taking the one fifty feet away.

We *must* make changes. Keeping our body in shape keeps us in better soul shape as well.

> Much of what we have considered aging is in reality disease and degeneration from inactivity, bodily abuse and neglect. We will dramatically change the way we age if we take much better care of our physical condition. A fit, healthy body provides a foundation for continued growth and improvement in the quality of our lives. Remaining active and physically fit will also help us maintain self-confidence and self-esteem, two ingredients needed to create a positive personal identity and to grow young while growing older.
>
> We should also aim for optimal health for social reasons. An aging society needs seniors who are vital, healthy and independent citizens. Our nation cannot afford aging in the conventional way with heavy reliance on treatment for degenerative ailments. Spiraling health care costs could impoverish the nation. If we care about the future of our country, we need to care about our physical well-being so that we don't add to the drain on increasingly scarce resources.[18]

Most adult deaths in our country are premature. They occur not because of old age or previously prevalent diseases but because of diseases of the heart, cancer, cardiovascular disease, cirrhosis, and accidents. Many are preventable.

Personally, I began exercising at forty, riding an exercycle ten miles daily until recently, stopping because of ligament damage in my knee. I also played racquetball two or three days a week for fifteen years. My resting heart rate went from eighty to sixty, and I had more energy than I did years before. At seventy-two I went to a gym and worked with a trainer for a year. Now I'm starting at another gym (thanks to a medical plan that covers the payment) and fast-walking my golden retrievers each day.

There are *many* exercise programs available—even some on cable or satellite TV. Benefit depends on quality and frequency; "irregular and moderate" doesn't achieve the needed results. Those who choose to improve their health discover they have more energy and agility. They also find new activities they'd thought weren't available to them at their age.[19]

Two key factors promote health: mental stimulation and exercise.

We're never too old to benefit from exercise, which seems the most nonmedical approach to improve and maintain health. Those who maintain the discipline for vigorous aerobic exercises are known for their longevity. Daily brisk walks for at least half an hour cut mortality rates in half compared with those not involved in exercise.[20]

What's more, your mental skills are better than you think. Too many who are older have accepted the antiquated thinking that our minds are going downhill. As Gail Sheehy wrote:

> Because most seniors accept outdated cultural poll studies about "dotty old people," they understand the mental skills, which are particularly high in reasoning and verbal expression, and try to evade intellectual tasks—exactly the opposite of what they should do to stay sharp. Their pessimism often leads to a premature and unnecessary dependence on others—spouses or children or their doctors.

People who develop the discipline of daily mental exercise read newspapers instead of only passively ingesting TV news, noodling over the crossword puzzle every day, keeping journals, balancing their checkbook, and reading the fine print on insurance forms, etc.—are preparing themselves. . . .

[They] can become distinguished today by belonging to the new aristocracy of successful aging. . . . [Their] added years offer an opportunity to display a great generosity of mind and soul, to forgive former enemies or to show dignity of conception in composing a thought, a poem, an expression of any sort that helps illuminate the path for others coming behind them. . . .

Your immune system needs to be signaled that you believe your life is worth fighting for. Again, even if you don't know what will give your life meaning at this stage, the very process of searching and working at it, every day, is a healing process, because it is opening up hope.[21]

Traits of Aging Well

"I can't change. I can't learn—I'm too old. . . . My brain has aged." Perhaps you've thought or believed or heard these statements. Whatever the case, they're myths. We once thought that after a certain age the brain began to decline and deteriorate. If cells were injured, that was it—they couldn't be replaced. We have learned that this is untrue.

A term that describes what does happen to our brain is *neuroplasticity*. "Neuro" refers to the nerve cells in our nervous system (e.g., "neuron"), and "plasticity" in this sense refers to what's changeable, malleable, or modifiable. Our brain can change, even when we're older.

A damaged brain often can reorganize itself so that, for instance, when one part fails, another part learns to substitute. If cells die, they can at times be replaced; many circuits or even basic reflexes we thought to be hardwired and permanent are not. Our brain can change its own structure and function through thought and activity. In other words . . . there is hope for your brain!

You might be thinking that you've been forgetting more and more, that you've been having those "senior moments," and that at your age you're the exception to learning anything new. However, it could be that you're not using the brain systems that regulate plasticity.

As children and adolescents we constantly were learning, and thereafter we learned new skills and abilities through work and other responsibilities. Then, though, for many years we mostly used what we'd already learned and mastered. This is a habit that we can, in some cases must, work to reverse.

Usually we don't become involved in tasks where we have to focus our attention as closely as when we were younger. So much of what we do is a replay of what we already know. We're prone to stick with what we've learned before, not adding to our knowledge and stretching the brain's ability.

Learning a new language in older age is one of the best things for improving and maintaining memory. It requires intense focus, which turns on the control system for plasticity, and helps in developing memory in other areas as well. Anything that requires focus will help.

My brother has completed a crossword puzzle daily for sixty years. I've learned not to play Scrabble with him since his vocabulary is so extensive. I continue to play the piano several times a week but search for new pieces and take "lessons" by listening to performers on CD and then using what I've learned to improve. Sometimes the muscles in my hands don't respond to what my brain is telling them, but in time and with practice they do get better.

More and more studies are showing how we can learn in our seventies and eighties. Auditory memory programs and other brain-exercise programs slow down age-related cognitive decline and lead to better overall functioning. Some have been able to turn their memory clock back ten to twenty years. There are even exercises to affect specific sections of the brain.[22]

We're deeply affected by our beliefs and attitudes. We could look at this and say, "I don't believe it" or "It won't work for me." How will you know unless you give it a real try? Remember: We have a choice as to how we age.

Age-Proof Your Mind is a book designed to detect early signs of memory problems. It shows not only how to counter them but also how to improve your memory and activate the brain's plasticity. "There are things you *can* do to tip the odds of memory presentation versus decline decidedly in your favor. You are *not* destined to become forgetful."[23]

Many resources are available if you'd like to investigate further. You have the choice. The brain will change; in which direction is up to us.

Since aging is part of our lives, let's consider the following:

Who ages best? Who desires the most from the experience of growing older? If we were to interview them, we'd hear some of the following:

They've developed an accepting view of others and themselves; they're able to forgive shortcomings. They don't keep grudges.

They're givers of their resources. They retain their passion to help others.

They have a concern about our world and the quality of the environment they will leave for the next generation.

They're reflective; they continue to understand and learn about themselves as much as possible.

They navigate their transitions well and grow through their experiences rather than getting stuck or regressing. They're willing to make changes within themselves and in their environment as best they can.

They simplify as they age in order to derive the most out of life. They set and can accept limits.

They're people of faith. Their relationship with God is essential.

Others seek them out for their wisdom, counsel, and insight.

They persist in self-study, classes, seminars. They refuse to stagnate.

Their lifestyle includes caring behaviors toward others and themselves. They've learned to take care of their bodies by eating well and exercising, and they can express their emotions genuinely.

They are people of hope, not despair, even in the face of much loss.

They have faced their mortality and accept that their death is coming.[24]

Those who age well have come to accept that life is both dreadful and wonderful. They learn to use their dark night of questions to let go of their own ideas of how things should be and to increase their faith in life and the love that undergirds it. They learn to accept—even welcome— ambiguity and difficulty because so many strengths can be cultivated during these times. They also know that the dark times will be balanced by times of playfulness, effortlessness, joy.

Many of us have not reached that level where we welcome difficulties. We sometimes feel lost in the darkness, plagued by doubts. We feel afraid around the mystery of what it all means and wonder if we could have avoided some of our suffering if only we had known better. To be aware that dangerous pitfalls exist and take every precaution to stay on safe ground is basic to claiming the harvest that comes with richly aging, but sometimes we need protection from life's disasters.[25]

Making (and Living) Our Choice

I've talked with a number of men and women between the ages of fifty and eighty about their lives. Some said they were satisfied and fulfilled with how they'd lived. Others looked back with regret and a sense of unfulfillment. Some feel as though their life is finished and yet unfinished at the same time.

Even if you feel fulfilled and believe you've completed what you wanted, do you still desire to have experienced something other than or more than you have? I've had and still have three occupations: professor, therapist, and writer. This has been and still is my life. It's me. I've loved what I've learned and experienced. But there *are* other things I'd like to have experienced too. Every now and then I'll reflect on, *I wonder what that would have been like.*

I also remember that what I've done for the past fifty years was not just work. It was a calling. Some of what I did and experienced wasn't a deliberate choice on my part. Sometimes I stand in amazement and say, "How did I get there?" I hope for more productive years even though I'm aware there's a better place coming where loved ones already await my arrival.

There's more to do and to experience. There are people to help. I have no sense of being indispensable—more so, while I have time and energy I want to train others to fill in and go further and do better. Perhaps this is part of leaving a legacy, helping the next generation of those called to minister in the name of Jesus. One step in this process for me was writing *Helping Those in Grief*, in which I poured what I'd learned over two decades into a resource that hopefully can be used to help others whether I'm here or not.

However, I do not struggle with tasks being unfinished or incomplete. There's another response: It's called acceptance of the unfulfilled/unfinished. When our vocation is over and finished, when time is gone and opportunities may seem lost, we will meet with the choice to accept the life we've lived.

There are those who believe their sense of fulfillment is tied in to their health and their time of death. At some point, though, we will need to accept whatever is or feels unfulfilled. There will be things we wish we'd said or not said, things we'd like to have heard, comfort we'd have liked to receive, forgiveness we'd want to have given or received. Nonetheless, part of getting older and being older is learning to live with incompleteness.

The other night I watched 8 *Seconds*, the movie about a champion bull rider killed at a young age. In one gripping scene, his father sits on a couch, filled with agony and grief over all he hadn't said to encourage or express love to his son. All his life the son tried to please his father and waited for those words of praise.

It's so common to experience this even if we *did* voice our love and acceptance. We still feel we fell short. I feel this way when I reflect on when my wife, Joyce, was dying of a brain tumor. *I could have done and said more.*

> The pain of unfulfillment is universal, the same for all. Even from childhood, consciously or not, man experiences his finiteness. It is a reality well calculated to make him rebel. He will either accept it despite everything, with a good grace or unwillingly, or else he will refuse it either in rebellion or in dreams. The attitude he adopts will control all his reactions throughout every stage of his life. The last stage, which is death, is only the acutest form of a problem pertaining to the whole of life.[26]

Acceptance—what is it? Some say "acceptance means you've got to." Others say it means "consent" or "resignation" or "you can't do otherwise." At any rate, acceptance is saying "Yes, to life in its entirety."[27] To accept means to choose the reality of what's occurring. That doesn't mean we always like it, but denying or fighting it won't lead to any changes. Throughout our lives we're constantly faced with choices to face reality instead of trying to put our energy into evasion.

Are you accepting your age, the changes in your life, the fact that you'll be older and different in ten years? Paul Tournier said,

> It is no easy matter to accept that one is growing old, and no one succeeds in doing it without first overcoming his spontaneous refusal. It is difficult, too, to accept the growing old of someone else, of one's nearest and dearest. The aging of a father whose judgment and advice always used to seem so sound, but whom one can no longer consult because he must not be worried, or because his faculties are failing. The aging of a friend to whom one no longer talks as one used to, because it would be necessary to shout out loud things that used to be said quite quietly. It is hard to accept the decay of conversation into banality, empty optimism and insignificance.
>
> Old age is indeed hard for the majority of people, and very hard for some. It must be said in all honesty. It is in fact one of those realities which must be looked at in the face.[28]

The process of letting go isn't about resignation. True, we used to do something we can no longer do, and we do things now we'll no longer do a few years from now. Here's the thing: We'll live differently, but we won't live less. Despite limitations, let's not overlook what we *can* do, and let's not fail to ask God to direct and guide our future. Yes, there is one!

> "For I know the plans I have for you," declares the Lord, "plans to prosper you and not to harm you, plans to give you hope and a future."[29]

> Call to me and I will answer you and tell you great and unsearchable things you do not know.[30]

There are minuses that arrive as we age, yet certainly there are pluses as well.

> You don't get old from living a particular number of years; you get old because you have deserted your ideals. Years wrinkle your skin, renouncing your ideals wrinkles your soul. Worry, doubt, fear and despair are the enemies which slowly bring us down to the ground and turn us to dust before we die.[31]

We can approach growing older in several ways. One is grasping the past and holding on. This could be refusing to relinquish a dominant or leadership role in a family or social arena, clinging to a job, wanting to be the influence, denying limitations, constantly informing others about accomplishments. Some dress like someone forty years younger or tackle strenuous events that others much younger and more capable would be hesitant to consider.

Another response is withdrawing into apathy and indifference. A person appears to have little or no interest in anything. Usually the frozenness moves into regret, depression, and even bitterness. Instead of moving forward, one who chooses apathy regresses and allows life to pass him by.

A third approach is choosing life—whatever that might entail. This is being present with (not absent from) life. The ambition is still there but now has been redirected. There's discovery of a new purpose and the setting of new goals. There is *meaning*, based in how we're living for the furthering of God's kingdom.

> Living with Jesus means living every detail of my daily life in that light. It does not mean detaching myself from the world and from the immediate concerns which give meaning to my life. I do not have to deny or oppose these provisional meanings of my life, but I shall be able to distinguish the transcendent meaning in every provisional meaning. Where is

God leading me in these daily events, in this ardor to achieve a goal that he has implanted in my heart, to this success, in this failure, in this joy or this sorrow, in affliction or this healing, this friendship or this rebellion, this light or this darkness? Meditation is just that—seeking the divine meaning in everything that happens to me, a familiarity with God that brings him into my life at every moment. It asks what is He expecting of me, here and now.[32]

Growing older means detaching from the past, and it means attaching to the present and the future. It's making a decision to choose life now and a future that will last for eternity.

10

A Reflective Life

One of our era's lost arts of is reflection. Some people aren't even sure what it is or how to do it. Part of the problem is reflection's pace: deliberate, unhurried. The concept runs counter to the times. Yet the older we become, the more significant reflection may become, sometimes in ways that surprise us.

You've probably used the term, but have you looked at its meaning? It comes from two Latin words: *re* denotes "back," and *flecture* signifies "to bend." Reflection on something is bending it back to take a closer look. Many find it exceedingly difficult to live reflectively, because it's so *slow*. Unless we reflect, though, we miss out on one of life's most important dimensions—the sacred, which, not coincidentally, is what gives life the most meaning.

What is sacred to you? Think about it. It could be that the only way we'll discover what's most sacred is by slowing down and bringing some of our tasks, events, activities, and commitments to a halt in order to reflect. Some of what's sacred will be different for each of us; some is the same for all of us (e.g., life itself is sacred).

For example, I've been highly influenced and impacted by one person. I've never heard him speak or spent time talking with him. I've met him just once. I've read everything he's written—some of his books several times. He changed how I view homeless people. He gave me a greater understanding of art. Through his book *Reflections on the Movies* I learned to always look for the plan or theme of redemption in films. His *The Reflective Life* prompted me to write about reflection and the sacred.

This man—Ken Gire—talked about an experience with his young daughter. The two of them were sitting in their backyard hot tub when she asked a question that, as he said, forced his system of values out of hiding.

"What are you doing tomorrow?"

If you were asked this by your child or grandchild or spouse, how would you respond? What thoughts would run through your mind?

"Oh no. I'm busy—can't change my plans. He/she probably wants me to do something. Why no advance warning?" Ever experienced such a response? Most of us have. We tend to intake questions like these not at face value but as though the other person wants to disrupt and infringe on our time.

Here's what Gire said:

> It wasn't a question really. It was an invitation. She was asking me to spend the day with her, but she didn't want me to feel the pressure to do it if I were too busy. Which I was. I was behind in my work and feverishly trying to catch up. But suddenly catching up didn't seem all that important. Not at the moment anyway. I knew something sacred was at stake in that moment. And though I didn't know exactly what it was, I knew what it wasn't. It wasn't my work.[1]

He then said he would take the day off and they would spend it together. She responded with "I'd like that," and he said he would too. They spent the next day on enjoyable activities. At the conclusion, his daughter said, "Ya know, Dad? This is one of those memories I'll treasure the rest of my life."

> As I reflected on what she said, I thought to myself, *I came so close to missing that time with her, missing making a memory that my daughter would treasure the rest of her life.* And I realized how many times like that I had missed over the years. Not just with her but with the other kids, with my wife, my friends, other members of my family. And the loss of those times, the loss of those moments in the lives of the people I loved and in my own life, made me sad.
>
> It also made me determined. To slow down, so I can see when those moments present themselves. To stop, so I can honor them. To respond, so I would not pass by those moments without in some way touching them and without them in some way touching me.
>
> Too many of those moments have passed me by.
> I don't want to miss any more of them.
> Life's too short.
> And too sacred.[2]

Life *is* too short. The older we get, the more we may believe it. There's never enough time left, whether or not there's much we want to accomplish.

Time is precious. Sometimes I ask myself, "Did I use my time well or misuse it? Was it wasted, or used wisely?" I feel this especially as I move through my seventies.

A Reflection in Time

Several years ago I wrote about the use of time. The research, study, and writing had more effect on my life than I'd expected. At that time I owned and directed a counseling center in addition to teaching graduate school and writing. I realized it was time . . . for me to close the center and stop my private practice. Doing this gave me the freedom to do something I'd wanted for years: go on a church staff and provide professional counseling as a ministry, not for payment. This is some of what I said about time then:

Think about how you possibly will spend your time in the future. Time analysts are now able to tell in advance how we make use of the time allotted to us. I wonder what we would do differently if we had known at an early age that we would spend 1,086 days "sick." The average person does. And you know as well as I do that some of our illnesses are preventable. Do you want to spend 1,086 days sick? Not likely.

You may be surprised that we spend eight months of life opening junk mail. Do you want to spend two years of your life on the telephone or texting or five years waiting in line or nine months waiting in traffic?

Just the basic necessities of life consume a large quantity of time. You'll spend four years cooking and eating. (You can't live on McDonald's, Burger King, and Taco Bell all the time. If we did, there's part of the reason for those 1,086 sick days.) You'll spend a year-and-a-half dressing, a year-and-a-half grooming, and (get this) seven years in the bathroom. Finally, the time experts tell us we'll spend twenty-four years sleeping and three years shopping.[3]

I don't know if all these calculations are accurate, but even if they are close we need to ask whether or not this is the way we want to use our time. At least this may help us consider how we use the time we have left.

Years ago someone wrote an article with an attention-getting title: "If You Are 35, You Have 500 Days to Live." Your first reaction might be, "Wait a minute, that couldn't be true!" Consider what the author said, though. When you take away all the time spent sleeping, working, doing odd chores, taking care of personal hygiene, taking care of personal matters, eating, and traveling—you end up with only five hundred days in the coming years to spend as you want. Isn't that sobering? It sheds new light on what the psalmist said, "Teach us to make the most of our time, so that we may grow in wisdom" (Psalm 90:12).

Tim Hansel raises the question of what you would do if you received a daily call from your bank saying your account had been credited with 86,400 pennies ($864) and that this money had to be spent that day. Nothing could be carried over to the next day, and when midnight hit, what you had left would be cancelled out. Would you let any money remain? It's doubtful. You would make sure every bit was used.[4]

In *It's About Time,* Leslie Flynn says you and I do have such a bank: The First World Bank of Time. Each morning the bank credits your account with 86,400 seconds. That's 1,440 minutes, or twenty-four hours. It's the same for each of us. And keep in mind that no balance is carried over to the next day. If you choose not to use it, you lose it. You can't accumulate it.[5]

How will you make wise use of your time? How will you take the investment God gives you and use it with purpose and meaning?

The New Testament uses two different words for time: *chronos* and *kairos*. Time governed by the clock is *chronos*; time measured by events or special moments is *kairos*. *Chronos* could include timetables and prearranged work schedules. Many find that most time falls into this category. *Kairos* is where life is experienced in the events—the special moments—of past, present and future—these are the sacred moments. Some experience this rarely; others never at all. Their lives are ruled by the clock. These people will take their five hundred days and govern them rigidly. But life is fuller when you occasionally overrule the clock and live in the special moments.

Scripture charges us to redeem time, to use it for all its worth: "See then that you walk circumspectly, not as fools but as wise, redeeming the time, because the days are evil" (Ephesians 5:15–16 NKJV). How are you going to redeem the time the Lord has given you?[6]

Now I'm in my seventies. I don't have those five hundred days left. I'm not sure how many I have, but I do know the type of time I'm more interested in experiencing. And it's not just a matter of emphasizing *kairos* to the exclusion of *chronos*. I still need some timetables, goals, and structure. The more flexible I am, though, the more special and sacred moments await me.

Selecting the Sacred

Many respond to the suggestion of spending more time in reflection with something like, "I'm not sure I could. How does one reflect, anyway? Is it just thinking? Praying? Constructing something else to do in my mind?"

Others say, "It's threatening to sit and reflect. I stay busy to cover my pain. I'm afraid to reflect much because I'm not that comfortable with who I am. When I reflect I see the real me."

Still others report, "I can reflect for a while, then my mind goes down a bunny trail, wandering away. When I try to pray I have the same problem."

Everyone can learn to reflect. Anyone can choose to confront their real issues. And we all have a wandering mind—it's easy to begin daydreaming, planning, fantasizing, or aimlessly drifting about.

But God knows and loves us anyway, and He doesn't want us far from Him.

> You, Solomon my son, know the God of your father [have personal knowledge of Him, be acquainted with, and understand Him; appreciate, heed, and cherish Him]—and serve Him with a blameless heart and a willing mind. For the Lord searches all hearts and minds, and understands all the wanderings of the thoughts. If you seek Him [inquiring for and of Him, and requiring Him as your first and vital necessity] you will find Him.[7]

Will you give some time to reflect?

Reflecting is thinking. It's meditating. It's asking questions of oneself about thoughts, beliefs, values, identity, goals, and, most of all, who God created us to be and wants us to be. It's pondering Scripture, looking deeper by considering, "What is this saying, and what does it mean for my life?"

This is why some people journal, so their times of reflection can also be times of clarification. It helps people see where they've been, where they are, and where they're going. Some journal specifically during crises so that they can move forward and be able to reflect again.

Following the death of my son, writing devotionals for several months assisted my understanding of the Word. Following Joyce's death, I journaled; in the midst of my grief, writing my struggles and feelings helped me reflect and to rediscover both clarity and purpose.

Prayer can be a time for reflection, especially if it allows God to do as much talking to us as we do to Him. Prayer is not meant to be a monologue. It's intended to be as much hearing as speaking, not a one-way process.

A reflective life is one that reflects this statement: "They delight in the law of the Lord, meditating on it day and night."[8]

When we take God's Word into our life and think about just one verse a dozen times daily, reflecting on how we'll live out this verse in an everyday way, we're reflecting *and* growing.

James Packer describes prayerful meditation as an activity of

calling to mind, thinking over, dwelling on, and applying to oneself the various things one knows about the works and ways and purpose and promises of God . . . of holy thought, consciously preformed in the presence of God, under the eyes of God, by the help of God, as a means of communication with God, his purpose is to clear one's mental and spiritual vision of God, and to let his truth make its full and proper impact on one's mind and heart. It is a matter of talking to oneself about God and oneself.

It is, indeed, often a matter of arguing with oneself, reasoning oneself out of moods of doubt and unbelief into a clear apprehension of God's power and grace.[9]

So, what is sacred in your life?

Perhaps it's time to ask not self but God what, in the years you have left, would He want you to make sacred. Regardless of what decade you're in, what might He be asking of you for the many or few years remaining?

It's not profound.

It's actually simple.

And it isn't even new.

We've heard it so much we ignore it or tune it out.

It's *relational*.

"Love the Lord your God with all your heart and with all your soul and with all your mind." . . . [And] "Love your neighbor as yourself." All the Law and the Prophets hang on these two commandments.[10]

We're called to live reflectively so that we can discover what's sacred in life no matter where we are along the way. So many people over the years have told me that what made the difference in their life was knowing they were loved. They know they were loved, they were shown they were loved, they were told they were loved. Who knows that you love them? How do they know?

My brother is seven years older than I am. We've been close all our lives. We know we've loved each other—we just didn't say it.

Several years ago that changed in a dramatic way. I was talking with him on my cell phone from Cedars-Sinai hospital in Los Angeles, waiting while Joyce had her second brain surgery. At the end of the conversation, he signed off with "I love you," and I responded in the same manner.

As I began walking back inside, I wept. It was an overwhelming gift to hear the words. Ever since that time, we have ended each conversation with them. Why didn't we share them before? I have no idea. However, we can't ever assume another person would just know we love them—our showing and our saying must be in wholehearted harmony. Ken Gire describes it so well:

> The closer I get to the end of my life, [this] seems the only question that matters: Is the life I am living pleasing to God?
>
> The question will keep you up nights. And it should. As we pull the covers to our chin and settle into our pillow, that's the question that should bring our day into the presence of God for His scrutiny. Did the life I lived today please you?
>
> How many things do we have to check off on our to-do list before we can say yes? How many questions . . . before we can be done with them all and drop off to sleep?
>
> Only one.
>
> Have I loved well?
>
> So it's the end of the day, and each of us is lying in our bed, reflecting. Have I loved well? Has love been the beating heart pushing through all my activities? Can it be heard in all my conversations? Seen in my eyes? Felt when other people are in my presence? Was the truth I spoke today spoken in love? Were the decisions I made today based on love? Were my reactions? My devotions?
>
> Have I loved well?
>
> If we can answer yes to that question, it is enough.
>
> It may not be enough for our employer. . . . [For] our fellow workers. . . . [For] all the carpools and committees and other things on our calendar.
>
> It may not even be enough for us.
>
> But it is enough for God.
>
> And that should make it enough for us.[11]

11

Alone Again

Alone.

Not a pleasant experience, especially after being married many years.

Widowhood is the conclusion of almost all marriages unless a couple dies together. The two simple words *"I do"* signify the start of a committed relationship designed to last throughout life on earth. "Until death do us part" seldom registers, initially, but when the day comes, whether quickly or in half a century, it's still the disruption of a life. A widower who'd lost his wife after being married forty-eight years said:

> In place of all the words of joy, there are others. "Goodbye" is a constant, whether I verbalize it or not. There's so much to say goodbye to. It seems endless. When something occurs, you think of going home and sharing it . . . but then certain words come to mind: "Not here." "Never again." The most difficult couplet occurs when someone asks how your spouse is or there's a phone call. You hesitate for a second before

saying what you hate to: "She died." You know it's necessary. You know it's true. But you wish it weren't. You resist
saying the words, but force them out. It's reality.

"Relationship with spouse" is at the core of most married
people's life and world. He or she is part of your identity
and affirms your identity as well. When a spouse dies, the
other spouse's sense of self and security is shattered. Each
partner helps the other define the world and what's in it.
This too is lost.

The identity change from *we* to *I* can be one of life's most
painful transitions. (The first time I saw my name listed as
"widower" I was taken aback.) Some of your friendships may
change, as many have been couple relationships and now your
time with couples will diminish. You'll need to build new relationships with people who share portions of your new identity.

What You Could Face

Whether you lost your spouse to a lingering terminal illness
or a sudden accident, your grief response will be similar. We
call the following "the crazy feelings of grief," but they're
actually a normal, healthy, sane response. Some grievers experience several; others experience all of them. How long
they last depends upon the type of death, the quality of the
relationship, prior losses, etc.

- distorted thinking patterns, "crazy" and/or irrational
  thoughts, fearful thoughts
- feelings of despair and hopelessness
- out-of-control or numbed emotions
- changes in sensory perceptions (sight, taste, smell, etc.)
- increased irritability
- no wish to talk a lot or at all

- lagging memory and mental "short-circuits"
- inability to concentrate
- obsessive focus on the loved one
- losing track of time
- increase or decrease in appetite and/or sexual desire
- difficulty falling asleep or staying asleep
- dreams in which the deceased seems to visit
- nightmares in which death themes are repeated
- physical illness (flu, headaches, other maladies)
- shattered beliefs about life, the world, even God

Grief will take longer than you've imagined. It tends to intensify at three months, on special dates, and at the one-year anniversary.[1]

You'll also experience additional or secondary losses created by the death of your loved one. If the death was traumatic, you may need to see a counselor to work through the experience's aftermath.

Secondary Losses

friend	provider
handyman	cook
lover	bill payer
gardener	laundry person
companion	confidante
sports partner	mentor
checkbook balancer	prayer partner
mechanic	source of inspiration or insight
identity	encourager
teacher	motivator

Secondary Losses	
counselor	business partner
protector	errand person
organizer	tax preparer
couple friends	in-law support
status	financial stability
social connection	feeling of safety

In addition to these concerns, others may look to you for help with grief: children, grandchildren, even older parents. There may be financial pressures to deal with. Adjusting to being home alone may become more difficult.

You'll have to contend with others' reactions. Some people will be intrusive and want too much involvement with you; others won't have much contact. At the same time you'll be confronting several major decisions, including the funeral, your spouse's business affairs, and your estate. (Two resources that may assist you are *Experiencing Grief*[2] and *Reflections of a Grieving Spouse*.[3]).

How You May Feel

What's it like to lose a spouse? He or she may have been your best friend. The *one* who shared a familiar mutual language, was your activity partner, gave and received daily physical contact. Maybe he or she was an anchor for you; now you feel cut adrift, even if your marriage was difficult.

Grief can make living seem like treading water without land in sight: you can't make sense of your surroundings, there's turbulence or even chaos all around, and you don't know how to move beyond fear and uncertainty to decide which direction to go. If you're alone, the following statements from widows and widowers may reflect some of your concerns and feelings.

- *"I'm angry."* You may feel abandoned. You could feel robbed of your future. You might feel like directing the anger at anyone, but it might be based in feelings toward the one who left, toward yourself, toward the doctor, toward whoever caused or is perceived to have caused the death (and so on).

- *"I feel guilty for things I did or failed to do."* Guilt also could arise over what you did or didn't say. Some people anguish over whether they provided well enough. Some wonder whether a different or better kind of care before the death may have helped.

- *"I feel old. And I think about my own death a lot."* The reality of one's own mortality frequently takes on a new meaning. Thoughts about death seem to surface consistently.

- *"I feel sick."* Many have health changes following the death. Oft-reported symptoms include insomnia, tiredness, anorexia, headaches, indigestion, chest pains, and heart palpitations.

- *"I'm afraid."* Fear (of driving, of shopping, of being alone, etc.) can become a companion, especially during the first few months after the death. Worries and anxieties seem to come out of nowhere and then multiply.

- *"I worry about money."* There's usually some financial upheaval following a spouse's death. All matters probably are not in order, and you may have little or no knowledge of the particulars. Maybe there wasn't a will (50 percent of property owners don't have one); income or assets may be insufficient; sometimes distribution is or seems unfair.

- *"I'm going through an identity crisis."* A wife can no longer call herself a wife, and a husband no longer a husband. Again, friendships with other couples will change;

the survivor will feel excluded. One young widow, filling out required information in the office of a new doctor, discovered there was no box to indicate her status. She said, "I'm not really married, and I'm not really single. If I had to choose, I'd have said married, because I don't feel single. I still have one foot in the marriage. It's only been fourteen months."

• *"I feel relieved" (after the death).* This normal response can come about for several reasons.[4] Perhaps the one who died had been terminally ill, suffered great pain, or lived with severe handicaps. He or she might have been an abuser or one who victimized others through chronic addictions.

This is what I felt a few months after Joyce died in 2007.

It's time. It's been a month since I've written anything. It's not that I haven't needed to write. Perhaps more than ever I do, but emotionally I wasn't into remembering. But this evening as I walked Shadow, my golden retriever, my mind drifted back to the beginning of this time in my life. It feels like the beginning of the end of a difficult journey. In my mind I see the trips and appointments and the visits to Joyce's oncologist and surgeons.

I've realized many things about myself as well as some uncertainties about me through this progression of grief. I wonder if there are times when I think or analyze too much. I know I ask too many questions that can't be answered. My grief is moving and changing. I'm in transition, which was bound to happen. Is what I'm feeling okay? Should it be at this level now? I'm not sure. Everything seems different and less certain.

The music I once listened to has a different effect upon me now. I know I've turned a corner, but that in itself brings a new set of losses. The memories aren't as sharp and neither are the images, which, in a way, are all I have left after such a loss. After almost fifty years together, shouldn't my feelings remain intense and vivid longer than this?

I'm discovering that I must have been carrying a low-grade grief fever during Joyce's illness. It was painful but recognized as such. Did I know or believe it would end like this? Not consciously, at least. I probably wouldn't allow myself to believe it. *Perhaps if I don't believe or think something, I can keep it from happening.* But magical thinking doesn't work, as much as I'd like it to. So part of me knew what was coming and a part of me wouldn't accept it.

I'm learning that healing comes when I reach out to help others. I've learned that I'm lonely . . . and I don't like being that way. I want companionship. I long for someone to converse with other than immediate family. But is that right? Is that okay? Where is the timetable of grief? Is there one? I debate what to do and say and which direction to go. It feels as though a part of me is stuck in the past, part is here in the present, and some of me is in the future.

Confusion reigns. Some say this is growth. I share some of what I'm thinking and feeling, but I'm not sure that everyone will understand and track with me. Yes, I know a lot about grief through my work, and that helped me during the first few months. But now I feel a bit more adrift and in the midst of uncharted waters wondering . . . sometimes just wondering . . . and waiting.

I'm finding a new sense of being out-of-control with my grief. I think I must have subconsciously had timelines constructed for where I would be in my grief at specific points. But grief refuses to be controlled. I'm still surprised by what happens and when it occurs, as well as when grief seems to have disappeared.

The future has changed. We tend to think of life as we've known it as never ending, forever ongoing. But grief drops a curtain over that belief.

What You Might Do

Anticipation of what's ahead has faded into uncertainty. Your old dreams included a companion at your side, and now there's an empty space. Your mind says, "He/she is with the Lord, I'll be all right," or "The future is still there and bright," or "I'll heal in time—I can do it." But your heart says otherwise; grief short-circuits the attempts of mind and heart to work together.

How do you envision the future when you're trapped in a fog? In order to do that you need to make forward progress and avoid being permanently stuck in a quagmire. Through the pain of contemplating next to that empty space, you'll need to learn how to direct energy toward considering that evasive future.

At the moment of a loved one's death, almost everything in us and around us changes. Or it seems to. We feel isolated. We may feel the world is now vast and confusing. We long for just a few moments with him or her. We reflect on the happiness he or she brought.

Nothing else makes sense because that rare and cherished relationship is gone. Consumed by devastating losses and aching longings, we see ourselves and others differently than ever before. *From this time on,* we think, *the world will never be the same.*

In a very real sense, your world *was* changed the moment he or she died. He or she has made up a precious and vital piece of your reality. At such a challenging time, you must be patient with the chaos you're enduring.[5] Realize: *We don't move forward when the grief concludes but while it's present.* And some of us will move in and out of grief for years even though we've built an entirely new life—that's normal.

You won't feel or be entirely the same way in three months, six months, or a year or two from now. What you do with your time, energy, and other resources will be different. (If you could foresee the future, too, you'd probably be surprised at how active and involved your life could be.)

You may not feel there's a future, but there will be . . . and you have a strong hand in shaping it. Maybe, right now, just getting through the day feels overwhelming, let alone considering the next month or the next year. But you will get (and grow) through, and the future is coming. Enlist the help of others—wise, compassionate, and supportive others—to assist you.

How can you face your void? You can broaden your roles and your skills. You can learn to function without your mate. You'll change what you do and take on or delegate the responsibilities your spouse handled. You'll give up some things and choose not to do others anymore. Adjustment means, in part, not behaving the same way as when your partner was here.

As one person said, "That portion of life is history. I will never be that person again." Moving on includes reinvesting your emotional energy. I'm not talking about replacing a former love—any attempt to make a replica is unhealthy. Instead, discover satisfaction and fulfillment through connection with a service organization, a ministry, a new career, a new hope, and so on.

One other thing: Recalling how a loved one died is normal and necessary. Repetitious reviewing helps you fully realize that your needs, hopes, expectations, and dreams of continuing to be with him or her won't be fulfilled. Each time you remember the death and its surrounding events, accepting the change—that you won't be together in the way that you were—your understanding will increase, and so will your strength.[6]

You *can* move forward. You *can* recover. Life won't be the same, but you *will* have a new life.

12

Married Again?

In the wedding ceremony we make promises. One phrase, "Till death do us part," we gloss over, and then it happens. Whether or not the reason you're alone is death, the question is, will you remain single or begin looking?

Many say, "I've experienced marriage, it was good, and that's it." Or, "It was terrible, and I'm glad to be done." Most start out planning to "live single." Within a few months, though, "maybe again" might enter into your thoughts about another relationship and remarriage.

In addition to everyone's unique situation, there are several possible combinations. For example, both are divorced and have been single again for some period of time. Or one is divorced and the other is a widow or widower. Or both individuals lost their spouses to death.

Usually, the post-divorce relationship with an ex-spouse isn't friendly; some people even hang on to or struggle with resentments and bitterness. The more children there are, the more haggling and disagreement can occur, which can influence everything from the ongoing details of your schedule to where you live. Some want to avoid involvement with the opposite sex for some time. Some focus entirely on the kids and vow not to look for another spouse indefinitely, or maybe until all the children are at least a certain age.

Remarriage can occur for healthy and unhealthy reasons. Either way, it can introduce a number of risks; for instance, debts, emotional baggage, and children can complicate the relationship. If you're marrying someone with kids, you're truly marrying a family, and after divorce many children are opposed to remarriage. Frequently they believe you should be with your former spouse instead of the new one.

> In general, remarriages (where one or both partners have been married before) with or without children have a 60 percent or greater chance of divorce. Specifically, second marriages have a 60 percent divorce rate and third marriages have a 73 percent chance of divorce. Remarried couples who bring children to the wedding have an even greater risk of divorce; to be specific, they have a 50 percent greater chance of divorce than remarried couples without children. As it turns out, happily ever after is tougher to achieve in remarriage, even more difficult when one of you brings children to the marriage, and especially challenging when you both do.[1]

Many a remarrying older couple believes they'll be free from problems or resistance from adult children who have their own families. No matter what age your kids are, though, they still will have opinions and preferences. Some believe that they'll be accepting if our decision is based on love. In any case, you cannot control how or what others think and do.

The attitudes and adjustments of the children can vary profoundly, and they might be or seem to be more about them than about your relationship. Some *will* welcome their parents' decisions and be delighted with their possible newfound happiness. Others will gradually adapt and accept. Some will resist and stand off for months or even years. In fact, I've seen some situations where all three possibilities exist within one family.

Whether the remarriage is after a divorce or after a death, even one that occurred years ago, previous hurts and losses reemerge. Fears of history repeating itself can surface and influence a new relationship. Many people are surprised by what they call a ghost of the past emerging and interfering with the present. Ungrieved losses can be particularly disruptive.

How did you relate to your first spouse? What were the constructive ways, and what were the destructive ways? What have you learned about yourself since your divorce? An originally destructive pattern will return unless you've endeavored to identify and deal with it.

Respecting One's Past

Every person who remarries has a personal history that contains hurts and sensitive areas. Examine yourself, learn what these are, and share them (whether or not they seem sane) with your new partner. In a second marriage a person might say of his spouse, "She's everything the first wasn't . . ." yet then add, "But at least the first one could . . ." Beware of comparisons. Your new spouse will be different. Even if you sought a replica of the first spouse and hoped "this time it'll turn out all right," he or she won't be the same.

Embracing Realistic Expectations

Each person entering a new marriage needs to have realistic expectations of self and of the new partner. Identifying and evaluating your expectations will go a long way toward eliminating disappointment and frustration. Some of your wounds can be salved by and even healed within this new relationship. Remember, if it was a divorce, the period of recovery often is three to five years. A divorced person must have time to grieve and deal with the hurts and losses. The opportunity to relate to a new person in a new way can have a markedly positive impact on your growth as you move forward.

Managing Contact With the Former Spouse

It's vital to consider and discuss the resources (especially time) to be given the former spouse and/or spouse's relatives in the event of either death or divorce. For instance, perhaps you'll have ongoing contact in the realms of kids, finances, or in-laws. The effects of conflict will be extensive if you carry unresolved issues or bitterness. This relationship must be conducted as a joint-parenting venture or even as a business arrangement. What will be invested—in what way(s), how often, through which means, and to what extent?

Making New Friends

How will you establish and maintain a world of new friends? Again, a divorce or death often involves losing a certain degree of previously shared community. Developing a support system within new friendships together could be a major task. Who will be the new marriage's social director?

"Resolve"

There are three big *R*'s to consider at this point. The first is, How did you *resolve* your relationship with your former spouse? (And how did your new partner resolve his or hers?) What's left over, negatively, from the old relationship will impede both individual and mutual growth.

Remember, in a remarriage there's an additional cast of characters. When I remarried I gained not only seven grand-children but also fifty new relatives. You marry your spouse's family and friends. Plus, both of you bring along already developed habits and routines that the new spouse is expected to accept (if not have known in advance!).

We all bring memories with us. When everything's going well, memories of the previous relationship are primarily negative; shortcomings are recalled. But when things aren't going well you may tend to focus on the formerly positive, even idealize the past. Remarriage is fertile ground for comparison.

Consider the following (some apply to divorce, some may apply to both divorce and death):

1. How did you try to work through problems in your previous marriage?

2. How did you relate to your previous spouse?
   What were the constructive ways?
   What were the destructive ways?

3. Who else helped in your attempt to work through your issues?
   What was beneficial?
   What wasn't beneficial?

4. If you have kids from the previous marriage, describe how you arrived at the plan of shared parenthood. How do you now feel about it?

5. Describe how much time and in what ways you spend thinking about your previous spouse. List your specific thoughts.

6. How often do you see your previous spouse, and for what purposes? What feelings do you experience on these occasions?

7. Describe how you confronted and handled your feelings during either the breakup of your previous marriage or the death of your spouse.

The remarrying person needs to have grieved both for the former partner and for the previous marriage. Grieving helps the pain of the loss to go away eventually. In contrast, denial dulls the pain of anger, which then becomes buried alive, full of energy.

Many would say they've worked through their feelings. Whether or not they have, these may return from time to time, and when they do they must be faced and experienced for what they are. Denying emotions prevents healing.

Events, dates, occasions, and places can bring back a flood of memories. What's wrong with you? *Nothing!* A new relationship's developments and changes and compel the past to surface. If it does, you have the opportunity again to face and resolve your feelings. It's important to discuss the process of adjustment with your partner without being threatened by the old relationship.

"Rebuild"

How have you as an individual attempted to *rebuild* since the divorce or the death of your spouse?

1. How long has it been since your previous marriage ended?

2. Who were the support people who helped you through that time?

3. How do you feel about yourself now as compared to how you felt at the end of your previous marriage?

4. What have you learned since the end of your first marriage (skills, relational habits, vocational changes, etc.)?

5. What did you learn from your past marriage that will help you in your new marriage? (For example, what have you learned about yourself—your needs, your feelings, your goals, your flexibility, your handling of stress? What are ways in which other people differ from you? How will you communicate and connect with your new spouse?)

6. How will you be able to be a better partner because of what you've learned? (Can you think of at least six ways?)

Guilt often becomes the second-marriage saboteur. Often unrecognized, guilt can appear to have no solution. Some think they have no right to build their new life on the wreckage of the past. Others feel they should simply remain thankful for (and "loyal to") a wonderful relationship.

As for the "emotional heritage" you will bring to your new marriage, at least five emotional responses usually emerge or manifest that are tied to the first marriage: fear, guilt, anger, jealousy, and resentment. Your fear might be, for instance, of having this new relationship also end in divorce or death. One man said, "My guilt came when I realized I was loving my new wife as I should have loved my first wife. If I had, perhaps it wouldn't have failed." Anger could stem from previous losses, from having so many demands to fulfill, from real or perceived slights, and so on.

"Rethink"

Specifically, what you'll need to *rethink* involves the developing of a new relationship. Is this occurring for healthy reasons? Are you on the rebound? Is desperate loneliness having a significant impact on your thought process? Are you making positive decisions based on wisdom?

At remarriage, one soon discovers there's no such thing as instant love or instant family. You've experienced a major loss and are hoping to have what formerly was lacking. But, to use just one example, you can be heavily occupied by the demands of children or of former in-laws. A stepparent may have just as much difficulty embracing a stepchild as the stepchild has with the new parent. Resentment can easily build as the new family struggles to accept one another and carve out the shape of a workable family unit.

1. How will you handle disputes over the grandkids' care and activities?

2. How do you feel about the types of gifts your former partner brings to the children or grandchildren?

3. What visiting privileges will you give relatives of your former partner who still relate to your children or stepchildren as part of their family?

4. What will you say about your new family when asked by others about the new relationships?

5. How do you plan to handle holidays, birthdays, and special occasions? How will you fulfill your desires, your new partner's desires, and the desires of the two families?

6. What will you share with your children about their expected response to or interaction with new relatives?

7. Describe how you've listened and responded to your children's concerns about your future (or new) marriage.

8. In what way have you included (or will you include) your children in the wedding ceremony, either by physical presence or by opinion?[2]

As for kids' involvement in a second-marriage wedding ceremony, there are several factors to consider. Children who've experienced a difficult divorce or the loss of a parent by death may find being involved a source of encouragement. They could gain the perspective that life can go on again, and being a part of the happenings might help them move forward.

The enjoyment and fun factor of preparations appeal to most children. When they take part in the service they have the feeling of helping their mom or dad. Even if they're not "in" the actual service, their presence should be acknowledged so they feel included. Often, when "Who gives this woman to be married to this man?" is asked, the children give the affirmative response.

Some couples take the honeymoon by themselves. Some include the children. Both can work out, but in either case, proper planning and detailed preparation is necessary.[3]

When there are grandchildren in the new family, a couple needs to organize time usage carefully. Sometimes a parent will spend time alone with biological grandchildren or children. The kids must know their parent-child relationship will remain regardless of the new marriage. It's also important that the new stepparent spends individual time with each stepchild and grandchild in order to build that relationship. Naturally, sometimes everyone will interact together (including the couple and both sets of children).

A divorced person who marries another divorced person may have numerous new conflicting-relationship factors. Consider just five the divorced man must contend with when he marries a divorced woman:

1. Former wife vs. new wife;
2. Children of new marriage vs. children of former marriage;
3. Kids of new marriage vs. kids of current wife's former marriage;
4. Former wife vs. children of former marriage;
5. Kids of current wife's former marriage vs. father of those kids.

Do prenuptial agreements have any place in a Christian marriage? It's rare to find these in first marriages, but in second or third marriages they're frequently considered. Some think such an agreement limits the depth of commitment to the relationship; others believe such a contract is necessary if there's substantial baggage brought from a previous marriage.

While it shouldn't be used to prepare the couple for or imply divorce, an agreement may help in certain cases, such as with certain savings accounts or with possessions intended for children of the first marriage. Kids, homes, investments, personal property, and potential inheritance may necessitate at least some clarification and/or legal agreement. Also, reviewing assets and obligations may bring to light other issues that had not yet been disclosed.

Items the couple needs to discuss and clarify prior to marriage include real estate, furniture/furnishings, stocks, money-market funds, and other financial accounts. In addition, the couple may want to have separate living wills or trusts. An agreement would itemize provisions each should make for the other in a will.

The basic expectation of a new marriage is that it will be different from—as good as or better than—the one that preceded it. That's especially true if the prior marriage had problems and ended in divorce or death. However, keep these facts in mind:

1. You can expect the second marriage to be more difficult to build than a first marriage.

2. You can expect it to be complicated, exasperating, and tiring.

3. You can expect it to be a slow-building process.

4. You can expect some "same old script" times even though you're writing a new script each day.

5. You can expect to want to run from it now and then (but you won't).

6. You can expect a lot of outside pressures that are new to you (e.g., from parents, children, families, jobs, and former spouses).

7. You can expect it to be successful if you dig in and go for the long haul instead of the overnight wonder.[4]

What's Next

Life brings many unexpected events and changes. In our wedding vows we say, "In sickness and in health until death do we part." But we don't really expect sickness and death to happen to us—that happens to others. But death does happen, as I experienced with my first wife after forty-eight years of marriage. For almost three years I was single again. But God is the God of new beginnings and new life. Once again I've been gifted with marriage and a special person. Tess is the new joy of my life, for she is a woman of beauty and Christian character. Once more I am learning about marriage and communication, not in my twenties as I first did, but in my seventies! You're never too old to learn.

13

Retire, or Redirect and Restructure?

Here are two responses to the transition of retirement. Can you relate?

When I finally decided to retire, my decision came quickly.

My husband, an Alzheimer's victim, had been in a convalescent home four and a half years. He'd started to lose his balance and was falling. I could no longer keep him safe at home.

My son had a seizure one night a year later and was diagnosed with a malignant brain tumor. The cancer had originated in his lungs. Shortly after that he was led to the Lord by a pastor. He had a valiant fight for eighteen months and died in 2007.

After his funeral, I took one week off and went back to work as a Marriage and Family Therapist. I felt I had to fill my mind with something productive and positive as quickly as possible. For the next two years I literally poured myself into my job, and when I wasn't working I had some good supportive friends

I spent a lot of time with. My life was extremely full, between them and visiting my husband every day after work. (By then he could no longer walk, talk, or open his eyes.)

There was no doubt my identity was in my work. I was enjoying what I did, working with people. In the meantime, the oldest of my three daughters was constantly badgering me, asking when I was going to retire. My fear was that, if I did, I'd no longer have my identity as an MFT and with time on my hands I might be overcome with grief for my son and my husband. Also, another big fear was that I wouldn't have enough money to live comfortably on with Social Security and my pension. That was not the case, I discovered.

I suddenly made a quick decision: I retired and soon was on a cruise ship with friends to Italy and Greece. I also spent ten days visiting friends in Florida and a month in Oregon. Contrary to what I'd feared, I found retirement to be totally pleasurable and have never regretted my decision.

Retirement resulted in what I refer to as *the great depression*, a loss so great it affected every aspect of my life. I left the best job I ever had at a time when it couldn't have been any better. I realized one day that the rewards of my work life had exceeded what I could imagine being possible. The depression lasted several years. At times I still miss the work experience I had, ten years later.

The challenge was in designing a new life for myself, one that didn't include being with my wife during the workweek because she still worked full time. I knew men who'd retired and ended up going back to work in some related capacity within the first year, out of boredom or perhaps a fear that their sense of worth was somehow tied to what they did in the world. For reasons I came to understand later, I didn't do that. I was essentially forcing myself to build a new life. It wasn't until later that I realized I was leaving the familiar behind because it would have become stale eventually, causing me to hang on to a livelihood that no longer invigorated my life if I'd stayed.

Designing a new life from scratch is a lot harder than staying in an existing job. Coupled with leaving a dream job behind and the support system I'd built within that job, I ended up feeling a great deal of loss and grief when I retired.

How We Got Here

Our present concept of "retirement" actually is a twentieth-century invention.

Through most of Western history (and certainly in other cultures today), people did not retire in the contemporary sense. There was no set toward-the-end-of-life leisure period one was entitled to in reward for years of labor. Most continued working every day and ceased only as their decreasing energy compelled them. As they aged and couldn't carry on as expected, they moved into roles of teacher, master craftsman, or counselor to younger workers.

One was never completely uninvolved in one's craft, business, or family farm. There was always work to be done, and with years only respective roles changed. "Retirement," if anything, meant a much shorter stretch when (or if) one was totally unable to work. Nobody wanted to be retired.

Whatever *our* primary role in life now, at some point retirement does become an issue, either by choice or by force. Hopefully we'll begin to plan for a point at which we'll step out of our routine and perhaps do only what we desire. *Retirement*, says *The Concise Oxford Dictionary*, means "withdrawal, or being out of circulation. Retreat, go away, seek seclusion, recede."[1]

Retirement has been described as a "roleless role." (Do you respond to that favorably or unfavorably?) One friend said retirement is the ending we both look forward to and dread. Some of us put it off as long as we can.

175

Nowhere does the Bible speak of retirement. While the Levites were told to relinquish responsibilities at fifty, they continued to mentor younger priests.

In 1899 German Chancellor Otto von Bismarck established sixty-five as the age at which his government would begin paying retirement pensions. Life expectancy was only about fifty-five at the time. He felt fairly safe about the guarantee.

In the United States, the Social Security Act of 1935 also set retirement age at sixty-five. This legislation was intended to ease older workers out, making room for younger, unemployed workers. Some saw it as a partial solution to the joblessness of the Depression.

With life's second half increasingly being extended, though, retirement for us can become a long, empty look into less and less. Dr. Howard Hendricks quotes Norman Cousins: "Retirement, supposed to be a chance to join the winners' circle, has turned out to be more dangerous than automobiles or LSD. . . . It is the chance to do everything that leads to nothing. It is the gleaming brass ring that unhorses the rider." He concludes,

> The reason is clear: There are two lines in a person's life: the lifeline and the purpose line. When the purpose line evaporates, it is just a matter of time before the lifeline ceases.
>
> What is clear from much of research on retirement is that how one deals with retirement depends in large measure on the meaning that work has for that person prior to retirement.[2]

Longevity means being as well and active as you can for as long as you can. It means staying engaged with life, taking responsibility for designing the future you want, remaining vitally connected to friends and loved ones and to society at large. The longevity concept is to be practiced during young and middle adulthood, when your body and mind are prepared for the long haul.

Dr. Dwight Small said of retirement:

> My personal struggle was to accept irreversible change and irreversible loss, factors very common in retirement. Accepting that change and loss without mentally turning back is the biggest challenge.
>
> One executive put it this way: "All I've got left is my future!" Another remarked, "I feel like I'm a missing person waiting to be found." A third wistfully quipped, "Ah, yes, I have a wonderful future behind me!" And from still another, "It's not exactly a picnic, this retirement thing!" We need to know which strategies to adopt if we're to turn a difficult transition into a skillful resolution.[3]

> "We live by losing and leaving and letting go. And sooner or later, with more or less pain, we all must come to know that loss is indeed a lifelong human condition."[4]

As Judith Viorst says, retirement comes with its own package of losses:

> Losing is the price we pay for living. It is also the source of much of our growth and gain. Making our way from birth to death, we also have to make our way through the pain of giving up and giving up and giving up. . . . And in confronting the many losses that are brought by time and death, we become a mourning and adapting self, finding at every stage—until we draw our final breath—opportunities for creative transformation.[5]

Retirement does involve giving up something. Tragically, though, some people simply give up. Furthermore, others may give up on us too.

One major adjustment for any of us as we move through life's "older" stages is facing the issues, real or imagined, of being no longer indispensable. Whether regarding work, church, or a family role, it's difficult to hear, "We're doing fine without you." This cuts to the core of what we've perceived to be our identity and purpose. Living in a rapid-change culture causes our past contributions to diminish or dissolve so that we cannot rest on them.

> Just when your self-esteem needs to be shored up by recognition of what you've contributed, those accomplishments lose their significance. We forget that those who preceded us felt the same loss when they moved on. . . . James Thompson of the University of Nebraska put it in a nutshell with his comment that retirement adjustment may be easier if one is a "never was" than a "has been."[6]

Though none of us wants to be forgotten, there are times when it feels as though this is exactly what's occurred. This feeling can peak after we retire.

A friend lived in a retirement community. One evening, when a large group of men met at the social center, he asked them to respond to the following two dreaded questions:

Who did you used to be?

I used to be a

  teacher

  nurse

  salesperson

  postal worker

  corporate executive

What did you used to do?

I used to

  teach

  care for others

  sell cars

deliver mail

make decisions

He said it felt as if he'd opened a can of worms as more and more of them began to share what they were experiencing. Before they left, he asked them to reflect on these questions:

Who are you now?

Who do you want to be?

What do you want to do now?

One meaning of *nostalgia* is "homesickness." From the Greek, the word itself means "to return home."[7] Whether we're young, or old, or anywhere in between, any of us can set up a dwelling place there. It also can refer to a wistful or excessively sentimental yearning for return to a past period or unrecoverable condition. Many who retire are hit with such longing.

From time to time we all escape to the safety of past memories. Some people, though, become captives. Certain attachments to the past can help us discern the future with greater wisdom, but others will limit our movement forward. The future carries with it a sense of uncertainty; the past is something we know for sure and can become a source of perceived security.

Sometimes, jokingly or seriously, we say, "Remember the good old days?" (which may not have been as "good" as we recall). Holding on that way limits us from making the present and future "the good new days." Nostalgia can distort; often it does so through exaggerated emotions.

It's common to feel that what we've left behind is not only people, roles, events, involvements, and experiences, but also us. True, we have left some of "us" behind . . . yet not all. We must participate in taking our current reality and turning it toward what's now and what lies ahead. As Dwight Small said, "Nostalgia can be terribly regressive in that it shuns the present and the future to feed on the past."[8] We want to have a hand in shaping what will happen.

Nostalgia is also tied to reminiscence. Why is it that as we age we're so prone to indulging ourselves this way? Think about it. Is it that we gain so much satisfaction from the memories, or that we use this to avoid looking at the future? It's probably some of both, but in the big picture, what else could it be that compels us consistently or even constantly to look backward?

In Peter Kreeft's words, "The experience of longing for the past that is unattainably gone is our deep nostalgia brought about by the knowledge of death. It is seeing our past with the eyes of death before we die."[9] Again, up until now, our past is us and we are our past. This is part of why, for many, nostalgic reminiscence hits when our work becomes part of our past history.

Jules Willing summarizes the problem as we face it at retirement:

> We have spent all of our working lives creating our own personal history, our eyes fixed on the future consequences of our acts and decisions. There has always been a next stage in our careers, the events of which we are formulating in the present. . . . But now for the first time we have reached the place where our story stops; there is no next stage. . . . For the first time, we can measure the entire distance from where we started a life-time ago to the farthest place we have reached.[10]

Our True Foundation and Calling

How will you handle this new phase? Or, how are you handling it now?

- Was or is work the primary source of your identity? If you were suddenly unemployed, would you still know who you are? Would you still be a person of worth? If you did lose your job, how did you feel about yourself?

- Have you believed work is inherently good, and thus the more you work, the better person you are? When you're letting others know how much you work, do you bemoan the long hours you put in?

- Do you feel you're not really serving the Lord unless you push to the point of fatigue? Do you ascribe to the idea that you'd "rather burn out than rust out"?

- Do you think the more you work, the more God loves you? When you imagine standing before Him, do you place your confidence in what you've done for Him or in what He's done for you?

- Did or do you feel indispensable? Think about what would happen if you couldn't work for several weeks.

- Did or do you control your work, or does it control you? Do you work in order to make a living, or are you living to work?[11]

Retirement isn't an end in itself, and it's not the end of life. Personally I don't care for the term. "Redirect" feels better, and it can be more accurate for many of us. In fact, hopefully you've noticed that's what this book is all about—*redirecting and reclaiming* our lives during this season of time.

In this interim "retirement" period, characterized by the increasing limitations of age, we have assurance that whatever God expects of us is achievable with the strength He gives. Age and time are not factors standing in the way. We're to manage all God gives us, including strength for the remaining time He allots us. He asks only that we be good stewards, faithful servants, Christlike disciples. Do you have eternity's values in view?

Interestingly, individuals who have a denial mindset often have no plans to retire—ever. It's as though by continuing in whatever they're now engaged they seek immunity from facing the end of all things earthly, including this life. But no one can forever escape the ultimate questions about the meaning of life's end.

Symbolically, never-ending work represents the continuation of the power to live on. "Person at work" it says, as though the maintenance of routine *gives* the power to live on. What an illusion!

One reason we struggle against the unfilled and the unfinished is our tendency to view this phenomenon in the category of personal failure. It's truly a mistake to equate success with tasks completed, failure with tasks not completed.[12]

How are we going to deal with what's left unfinished, we who know the Lord? Let us look to the apostle Paul as our example, for when he reached his ministry's finish he could say,

> As for me, I feel that the last drops of my life are being poured out for God. The time for my departure has arrived. The glorious fight that God gave me I have fought. The course that I was set I have finished, and I have kept the faith. The future holds for me the crown of righteousness which God, the true judge, will give to all those who have loved what they have seen of him.[13]

14

Your Purpose Now

Ever been lost in unfamiliar territory? I have, and I can attest that the fears and anxieties it yields make for an unpleasant experience.

Once, while hiking, we were trying to shortcut around a lake to save miles but instead ended up adding distance. Some people describe their trek through life's second half with similar words: *confused, weary, disoriented . . . lost*. Their sense of not being on the path they're looking for often is tied into purpose: "What's my purpose at this point? What can I do? Who can I be?"

Though we can misplace our sense of purpose, we also can rediscover or recreate it. Jack Nicholson portrayed a poignant illustration in the film *About Schmidt*.[1] A conventionally successful, pragmatically conservative actuary who retires after a full career with a firm in Omaha, Warren Schmidt instantly wonders who he is, what he's meant to do, how his life has significance.

Successive changes undermine his sense of self. Reaching retirement age has taken away the role he identified with why he mattered. Then his wife, who he cared for but wasn't close to, suddenly dies. His daughter, from whom he'd been emotionally estranged, already had moved away; now she's preparing for a marriage he's convinced will be a disaster. As he realizes he doesn't have a relationship with her that, from her perspective, warrants his input (much less his authority), Schmidt feels adrift, empty, detached, aimless.

It seems there's nothing he enjoys doing. He doesn't feel connected to anyone. But he has begun to write to and support Ndugu, an orphan in Africa, and when a caregiver writes back on Ndugu's behalf, attaching a painting the child made for him, Schmidt is deeply moved. He weeps as his soul is touched and as he faces questions he's been avoiding. What type of life has he lived so far? Has he really loved others? Has he been loved? *Is* there still purpose? *Can* he make a difference? *Will* he discover something to live for?[2]

Purpose gives us vitality, fills us with life. Purposelessness leads to death, for it overshadows life itself.

Without something to live for, we die. With something to live for, we experience the second half of our lives with meaning and purpose. Purpose is one thing that cannot be taken from us. Our purpose is, ultimately, the something we live for. It is the quality or thread we choose to shape our lives, at all of life's stages.

There comes a time in all our lives, though, when time is of the essence, when our "life spiral" is spiraling out and we no longer have forever to live. We must put our whole selves into life, now. Admitting that is the first step, and quite a first step it is.

But our path forward can be seen more clearly.

One of the things we love about the people we've known who have exemplified the most vital kind of aging is that they have found strength and joy in self-acceptance. They know and respect who they are, and they've discovered a means of engaging with the world that allows them to express themselves and that gives them joy.

We invite you, then, to sit quietly, for a moment, and envision yourself as an elder—imagine yourself at, say, age one hundred.[3]

Don't Leave Home Without It

Another movie I enjoyed, based on a same-titled novel by Jim Stovall,[4] is *The Ultimate Gift*. In a sense it's about a man who accepts the inevitability of dying and has made friends with death while still experiencing life and leaving a legacy. James Garner portrays a billionaire who forces his grandson to learn the value of helping others before he can receive his inheritance; as he learns there's more to life than money, his grandfather gives him a number of gifts in the form of lessons. This is what the older man wanted to be remembered for—this was his purpose. What are the lessons you've learned and can pass on to others?

The concept of "never enough" resides in most of us. Some would admit to it, whereas others deny its presence. Honestly, who wouldn't want more of whatever brings the most satisfaction or delight? Some people feel a constant, nagging sense of dissatisfaction that diminishes the benefit of what they've received. Others want "more" because what they've experienced has been so wonderful that they want it to continue or return if possible.

One person's purpose can impact *generations*. But sometimes we wonder if we couldn't have done more, if there's any way we truly can have "done enough." Perhaps we think we haven't fulfilled God's purpose for our lives. *Saving Private Ryan*[5] sent me down this pathway.

In the movie, a squad is deployed to locate and bring home one soldier whose brothers have all lost their lives; he's his mother's only surviving son. Though eventually they find him, several are killed in the mission, including Captain John Miller (Tom Hanks). Dying on a bridge, after the battle has been won, he whispers to Private Ryan, "Earn this." . . . *Earn this.*

James Frances Ryan goes through life with these words ever ringing in his mind: *"Men died for you. Live up to their sacrifice for you. Don't let your life be wasted—it was bought by the blood of others."* (How like our redemption that was proclaimed by the blood of another—Jesus Christ.)

In the end, the now-elderly Ryan takes his family to visit his captain's gravesite in Europe. His face reflects both his memories and his feelings; he wonders, *Did I earn this? Did I do enough? Could I have done more?* As his wife walks up to join him, he turns and says, with a painful expression, "Tell me I've led a good life. Tell me I'm a good man." Perhaps those thoughts had haunted him over the decades. Maybe he asked these of himself thousands of times. But now he voiced them; he wanted, needed, to hear the affirmation. "You are a good man. You did earn your life." *You did fulfill your purpose.*

We all have "self questions," questions about who we are, who we could be, what we could have done, what we'll be able to do. These reflect on our purpose. In *The Purpose Driven Life*, Rick Warren suggests five benefits of having one and says, "Without God, life has no purpose and without purpose life has no meaning. Without meaning, life has no significance or hope."[6]

We *need* hope. What's the degree of hope in your life right now?

When we know our purpose, we can simplify. We can sort out what's important and what isn't. Running your activities, opportunities, and tasks through the grid of your purpose and then eliminating clutter can bring peace.

> You, Lord, give perfect peace to those who keep their purpose firm and put their trust in you.[7]

Your life gains focus with purpose. Instead of being exceedingly busy while going nowhere, rushing and scurrying without accomplishing what's most needed and wanted, you'll be able to use the energy and other resources once devoted to the unnecessary for what matters most. You'll be motivated to fulfill God's purpose for your life through love and service.

Knowing your purpose will better prepare you for the future in eternity. And this is the primary legacy we can leave, an everlasting one. We're not here to be remembered, and most of us won't be. Warren suggested that when we get to heaven God will ask us two questions: "What did you do with my son, Jesus Christ?" and "What did you do with what I gave you?" Now would be a good time to consider and answer these.[8]

Purposefully Changing (and Following) Directions

I hear people experiencing what could best be described as regrets. "I wish I had . . ." or "If only . . ." Many express these in regard to a loved one no longer with them. Others do so about issues in everyday life, or dreams that died, or opportunities or experiences or relationships that didn't materialize.

> Living our unlived life is the most important task in our mature years, to be achieved long before a tragedy shakes us to the bone or we reach our deathbed. To live our unlived life is to become fulfilled, to bring purpose and meaning to our existence.[9]

There's that word again: *purpose.* We truly don't want to try living without it, and if you've been missing it, there's no better time than now to begin seeking and embracing it.

Every person's life slips into the "unlived" category in some way or another. Can you think of something in yours?

What might have been abandoned or unrealized? Was there a talent never nurtured to its potential? Further, have you ever considered that when we choose something there's also something we didn't choose?

One woman asked, "How do I know what was unlived?" Perhaps it's whatever already seems to you to be missing. If you've felt this, what might that be—can you define what it is? How is this impacting you—how are you thinking and feeling about it at this point in your life?

> If you don't do something with the unchosen, it will set up a minor infection somewhere in the unconscious and later take its revenge on you. Unlived life does not just "go away" through underuse by tossing it off and thinking that what we have abandoned is no longer useful or relevant. Instead, unlived life goes underground and becomes troublesome— sometimes very troublesome—as we age. Of course no one can live out all of life's possibilities, but there are key aspects of being that must be brought into your life or you will never realize your fulfillment.[10]

This statement reminds me of what so many of us do with hurts and losses: bury them underground. Again, though, they're not put to rest but buried alive. They have the ability to attach themselves to new hurts and losses and infuse them with more pain. Leaving these underground means that when they stir and are resuscitated, you won't be in charge of them.

Unfortunately, this process happens often with abused children, since for some it's the only way they can handle the injuries inflicted. What's become buried then interferes with the rest of their lives. In time they will need to revisit what was boxed up and discover a way to release its presence.

Whatever your age, wherever you are in life, you have the opportunity to explore not only your unlived portion but also what yet can be discovered and lived. The rest of your life, however long, can be lived to the fullest.

It's easy to get lost. For some of us, when (not if) that happens, it throws us into a panic. Most of us want to feel and believe we're in control of our lives. Especially difficult is the attempt to navigate somewhere you've never been.

For literal navigation, fortunately, technology has devised a (nearly foolproof) satellite-based solution: GPS, or Global Positioning System. Program in your destination and let the system guide you there; it works if you follow the instructions. Sometimes we think we know best and ignore a directive. That's when the voice proclaims, "Recalculating route," which it then does.

Many attempt to live without a guidance system of any kind. Many more subscribe to one but pick and choose its directions. I've seen drivers actually argue with the GPS voice. While that part was humorous, what wasn't funny was that their attitude ended up getting us first off course and then, usually, lost. Some even chose to dispute the next set of instructions and thus caused us to waste additional time.

Refusing *or* ignoring wise guidance leads to navigational crises. Spiritual and emotional "GPS" is crucial in life's later stages, as "recalculating route" is what we're already involved in doing. What's your guidance system? In our own wanderings, self-reliance in the face of accurate guidance is a slippery path down a steep grade.

Are we stubbornly clinging to our inadequate solutions because we're afraid of making mistakes? Let's face it, failure *is* part of life, and our errors don't ever surprise God. He knows we're imperfect and that we'll fall short, and He loves us anyway. That's good news in this hyper-competitive world!

Some failures involve sin; some don't. Regardless, God has promised to never leave us, forsake us, or turn away from us.

The Lord is close to the brokenhearted
and saves those who are crushed in spirit.[11]

The Lord upholds all those who fall
and lifts up all who are bowed down.[12]

And, God sees *beyond* our failures. We say, "Look how I've blown it. I can never serve effectively again." God says, "So you've blown it. Let's discover what you can learn and then put it to use for my kingdom."

Purpose With Passion

Everyone has struggled. Isaiah lamented, "I have labored in vain; I have spent my strength for nothing at all."[13] Job groaned, "My life drags by—day after hopeless day. . . . I give up; I am tired of living. Leave me alone. My life makes no sense."[14] Yet no matter what we feel in a given moment or during a given season, our identity and purpose at any age comes through relationship—not specifically with a friend or mentor or parent or spouse or anyone here, but directly with Jesus Christ.

> It's in Christ that we find out who we are and what we are living for. Long before we first heard of Christ and got our hopes up, he had his eye on us, had designs on us for glorious living, part of the overall purpose he is working out in everything and everyone.[15]

One of the differences between being young and being older is what we know (or think we know). Early on we think we know so much and that every question we have will be answered. Older, we realize we didn't know as much as we thought we did and that many questions may not be answered.

Even so, as Warren reminds, we can share and give from our experience:

What are the major lessons you have learned so you can share them with others? We should be grateful Solomon did this, because it gave us the books of Proverbs and Ecclesiastes, which are filled with practical lessons on living. Imagine how much needless frustration could be avoided if we learned from each other's life lessons.

Mature people develop the habit of extracting lessons from everyday experiences. I urge you to make a list of your life lessons. You haven't really thought about them unless you have written them down. Here are a few questions to jog your memory and get you started:

- What has God taught me about failure?
- What has God taught me from a lack of money?
- What has God taught me from pain or sorrow or depression?
- What has God taught me through waiting?
- What has God taught me through illness?
- What has God taught me from disappointment?
- What have I learned from my family, my church, my relationships, my small group and my critics?

Your life message includes sharing your godly passions. God is a passionate God. He passionately *loves* some things and passionately *hates* other things. As you grow closer to him, he will give you a passion for something he cares about deeply so you can be a spokesman for him in the world.[16]

What are your *passions*? They may yield insight into your purpose.

Dr. Paul Brand, who co-authored several books with Philip Yancey, talked about his missionary mother, whose board said it was time to retire when she was sixty-nine. She was ready to do so until she discovered another group of people, high in the mountains of India, who'd never heard of Jesus. What followed wasn't easy, but she had a calling and a purpose.

Without mission society support, she climbed those mountains, built a little wooden shack and worked another 26 years. Because of a broken hip and creeping paralysis, she could only walk with the aid of two bamboo sticks, but on the back of an old horse she rode all over the mountains, a medicine box strapped behind her. She sought out the unwanted and unlovely, the sick, the maimed and the blind, and brought treatment to them.[17]

Brand remembers her this way:

Granny's own rheumy eyes are shining, and standing beside her I can see what she must be seeing through failing eyes: intent faces gazing with absolute trust and affection on one they have grown to love.[18]

This woman, still an active servant into her mid-nineties, followed her purpose wholeheartedly and made a difference.

It is [God] who saved us and chose us for his holy work, not because we deserved it but because that was his plan.[19]

You were chosen to tell about the excellent qualities of God, who called you.[20]

The Primary Purpose of Purpose

When you serve God and others, you *are* doing something significant, and this is a purpose we all have—we were chosen for His work and to tell others about Him. *How can you reflect that calling at this time?* How might you be used by God now? What interests you? What interested you years ago? Some things you may still care about, while others no longer have a claim. Is there something for which you have a passion at this time?

Whatever gift or ability God has given you, it's for a purpose, and He wants you to use it the best way you know how.

What does God want you to do at this stage? Take the time to discover what He's gifted you for and desires for you; as Paul says, "Don't act thoughtlessly, but try to find out and do whatever the Lord wants you to do."[21] At the same time, "Try to have a sane estimate of your capabilities."[22]

The best way to serve God is to serve others. This, not self-service, is what we've been created for. Perhaps one of the ways to spend the rest of your life is, upon waking, asking, "Where and when am I to serve today?" Look for the answer; it could come in an unexpected or strange way. Whether it's a vacation day or a task-filled day, ask the question and anticipate being used.

Asking this question and following the answer has a lot to do with your attitude and your openness to learning how to respond in new ways—no matter your age. What you do now could be from home, in your area, or in another country. When I fly, for instance, I make sure I've brought several copies of *Experiencing Grief*. I've so often run into people in grief that I see sharing the book as an opportunity, and now I pray for that chance to minister.

When the word *mission* or *missionary* is mentioned, most of us relax and think, *That's someone else*. Most of us conjure up images of a certain type of person with a certain look and personality and plan. Conversely, the belief *That's not me* really needs to be changed to *That's me!*

Each person has been made for a mission—we're to serve God and to let others know who Jesus is. Paul puts it well: "God has given us the privilege of urging everyone to come into his favor and be reconciled to Him."[23] Note those key words: *given, privilege, urging, everyone, reconciled*.

What would you say if someone came up and said, "What's your life message?" If you've not yet thought about it, give it a start! I would answer with the motto I learned and committed to at the college department of the First Presbyterian

Church in Hollywood: "To know Christ and to make Him known." Their tenet was based on this passage:

> I want to know Christ and the power of his resurrection and the fellowship of sharing in his sufferings, becoming like him in his death, and so, somehow, to attain to the resurrection from the dead.[24]

Those of us who followed this creed expressed it in various ways. One became a seminary professor in Germany. Another is an astute businessman known for his high standards of ethics. Another founded the missionary organization Russia for Christ. Someone else taught in an inner-city school. My calling was to teach, write, and counsel, first in the area of marriage and family and then in grief and trauma.

What does God care about you caring about? And perhaps that's not the biggest question—maybe I should ask, How are you caring about what God cares about? What you've learned and done so far is your life message so far; God can speak to others through it.

Are you following His purpose for your life? Are you doing it wholeheartedly, as Caleb did? Whether or not you have done so up to now, *you can*. Whether or not doing so adds more years to your life, it absolutely, certainly will enrich the ones that remain.

15

The Legacy You'll Leave

Each of us, right up to and through this very moment, is creating our own legacy. Some of us have been doing this for many years.

As Tim Kimmel puts it, in his excellent book *Legacy of Love*,

> Your words, your schedule, your choices, your obedience, the way you savor your victories and the way you swallow your defeats all help to define your life. It is this definition that your children rely on most as they seek to chart their own future.[1]

What are others receiving from you? What are you giving to make your family great? What have you already given?

When it comes to leaving a legacy, there's a sense in which none of us has an option: We all leave one wherever our feet have touched as we've walked through life. However, we *can* choose what kind of legacy we leave. What you do, what you say, who you are will live on.

What will your legacy be?

I'm enthralled with a story Kimmel tells about traveling around the Bahamas by sailboat.[2] As he and his wife were snorkeling reefs and checking out isolated islands, they headed into the harbor of Man-O-War Bay for supplies and repairs. There, exploring inland, they stumbled upon a graveyard—a beautiful spot with tropical plants and flowers and a white beach in the background. But they were puzzled by open graves, which had apparently been dug months before. They'd never seen anything like it.

Returning to the harbor, they met a pastor and inquired about the graves. He said that because the island rested on a coral platform, digging a grave required several days. There were limited facilities and refrigeration; a body could not be preserved that long. People usually were buried within a few hours of dying, so the government required that two graves be kept ready for the next death.

Kimmel asked how, then, they could assemble people for the funeral. The pastor's answer was fascinating. In the case of a sudden death, they did the best they could to get people together. When there was a lingering or terminal illness, though, the funeral was held in advance.

When people were dying, family and friends would carry them into the church or come to their house for the service. (Have you imagined attending your own funeral?) Most times it worked out well and gave opportunity for the dying to hear what others had to say. And, sometimes, the people recovered. I wonder if hearing their own eulogy in advance—whether good or bad—may have encouraged them to keep on living.

Would you want to hear yours before the fact? Do you, as I do, wonder what would be said? What would you want your friends and family to express? What would you change today so that they would be able to speak of the influence you'd had upon their lives?

One Cherished Legacy

When my mother entered her seventies, instead of seeming to slow down she began to travel. She took six different world tours. Once, she helped smuggle Bibles into Russia!

Finally, in her eighties, Mom sold her homes and moved into a retirement center near me. Even into her nineties she continued to raise the flowers she'd always loved. She also continued to develop her ability in oil painting.

At age ninety, she concluded her own written life history with this poignant description of the center:

> When I first moved here, I attended all the activities (such as trips and concerts) and had so many friends. By 1989, I lost virtually all my friends to death and now, along with crippling arthritis, I feel very lonely here. Where I'll go from here only God knows.

For years my mother recorded her life experiences. My older brother, a writer by trade, compiled her material, supplementing it to include many other events and pictures from 1910 to 1990, and we gave it to her on her birthday. This was passed along to our children and to many other relatives as well.

Here was a woman whose values reflected both her early years and her family's background. Wanting us to develop our potential to the fullest, she encouraged us, helped us in any way possible when we struggled, corrected us when necessary, and demonstrated compassion. Mom passed on a strong legacy, a rich heritage from her side of the family. As a result, in a world where clear sense of family has been markedly fading, my brother and I have a better feel for who we are individually and as a family.

I heard the story of one event in our family's history, which happened at the reading of a will. The following is my description of what happened.

The seven family members huddled together, talking in hushed tones, the surrounding room reflecting the owner's many experiences. Sounds died out when a man holding a briefcase came through the door. As he sat in a chair, facing the others, all eyes were focused—he was the bearer of either good or bad news. He was the distinguished, gray-haired family attorney who'd summoned them together.

Those awaiting the reading of a will often are filled with conflicting emotions. Usually there's grief over the loved one's loss, blended with guilt or anger over unfinished aspects of the relationship, and also hopeful anticipation of what might be revealed in the will. Always there are personal expectations, whether or not we admit them. These seven survivors were no different.

After customary condolences and preliminary statements, the attorney began to read, thankfully brief and to the point. The shares for the four children and the three grandchildren were equal. But what the will stated wasn't what anyone expected. There was no mention of tangible material goods, and their absence left the seven wide-eyed. The words reflected a deep wisdom that would take time for anyone to fathom.

Since I love all of you, I want you to receive the best I have to offer. That won't be found in items or possessions or money. There is really no need for this will to dispense what I have for you, since it has already been given but perhaps not yet received or understood.

I have spent a lifetime of creating and giving to each of you. There's a legacy which each of you have received. It would be clouded and even contaminated by any of my material goods. Hopefully what I have left you over the years in our interactions and experiences will fill your lives more than what I acquired.

I have dispensed all my material wealth to the poor and homeless in your names. Now you will be free to experience

*the blessings of that act, as well as discovering what you
were given over the years. And when you realize what it is,
consider what you will pass on to others.*

If you'd been there, how might you have responded? Perhaps the intent is reflected in these words:

As each of you has received a gift (a particular spiritual talent,
a gracious divine endowment), employ it for one another as
[befits] good trustees of God's many-sided grace [faithful
stewards of the extremely diverse powers and gifts granted
to Christians by unmerited favor].[3]

The Ethical Will

Earlier I spoke of a film called *The Ultimate Gift*, in which a
wealthy man bequeaths "life gifts" rather than tangible ones to
his grandson. More and more elderly folks are choosing to do
exactly this. They want what they leave to their heirs to become
more than finances, more than material goods, something to
be used for the good of others as well as their offspring.

Some are deciding to create and leave an *ethical will*. This
can be a letter/document, a piece of artwork, a video, etc.
The purpose, no matter the format, is to inform the recipients
what you want them to have or to know or to be. It can be
in the form of a blessing, a teaching, a life lesson, a message
about significant values. An ethical will is designed to pass
on accumulated wisdom so that it doesn't die with you. It's
what you've learned about life that you believe is worthwhile
to hand down.

Dr. Andrew Weil strongly advocates this will's power and
purpose:

You can and should write an ethical will. You can choose to
share it while you are alive, or leave your thoughts for your
loved ones to share after you are gone. Regardless of your

199

age, an ethical will can be an exercise that makes you take stock of your life experience and distill from it the values and wisdom that you have gained. You can then put the document aside, read it over as the years pass, and revise it from time to time as you see fit. Certainly, while an ethical will can be a wonderful gift to leave to your friends and family at the end of your life, its main importance is what it can give you in the midst of life. . . .

An ethical will helps us harvest the wisdom of the first half of our lives to more generatively shape the second half. Maggie Kuhn, the indomitable founder of the Gary Panthers, urges us to do something similar in what she calls a "life review." A life review inspires us to realize the ways we have coped and survived in the world through the stories by which we define ourselves.[4]

So, in an ethical will, you recite for posterity not only a summary of your life but what you've learned, valued, and believed, emphasizing qualities (say, trustworthiness), characteristics (concern for social justice), and passions (savoring sunsets over the ocean or mountains) you wish to pass on, revealing your hopes and dreams for those who survive you. Perhaps in given cases you already share a particular affinity or trait with this or that loved one, or you've observed it in him or her but haven't previously disclosed your perspective or insight. You may share what you regret doing or weren't able to complete.

You could add a section about special and influential people or events that impacted you ("From my parents I learned . . ." or "I'm so grateful for [experience/event] because [list the benefits]"). You may wish to "bequeath" to a son or daughter (or someone else) one of your qualities or pass along to a spouse one of your passions. Your ethical will, with your life story, can become part of your family's heritage, passed from generation to generation.

You may choose to write a general ethical will to all those you care about. You may ask that it be read at your funeral or printed in the funeral program. Another option: specific ethical wills to different categories of people, such as one to your children, one to your grandchildren, one to your parents, one to your siblings, and so on.[5]

I asked a friend, "What's the legacy you hope to leave for others?" He replied,

> That of never giving up and never to stop trying, as life is a little like riding a fabulous horse. . . .
>
> There is nothing more exciting than galloping across the country, but staying centered is the most important thing you can do—it prepares you for both the big and little things that can happen. If you're not centered and the horse stumbles, chances are it will throw you . . . and if it does, you've got to get up, dust yourself off, get back on, and ride again but stay as much as you can within your riding abilities. . . .
>
> Keep training and learning so you become the best rider that you possibly can be in this thing called "life."

Have you heard of or read the poem "The Dash" by Linda Ellis? I've heard portions of it at several funerals. Most of the time the words and purpose are similar. At the graveside part of the service, the pastor mentions the date of the deceased's birth and death, but those dates weren't the most significant part of their life. What mattered most was the time between those two dates. What matters most is how we live our life.[6]

16

The Last Chapter

I read novels. I've been reading them ever since I learned to read. I love the way I can project myself into the story and see it in my mind. There are times I've enjoyed it so much I very much wish the book weren't coming to an end. On other occasions I can't wait to arrive at the last chapter to see what awaits.

Life is full of chapters as well. As Paul Tripp writes, it's "much like being in the middle of a novel."

> Every day you are faced with things that were not part of your plan. . . . You get wind of massive changes in the company you work for, and you wonder whether you will be one of the long-term employees to be furloughed. Or you are watching one of your grown children make a rather chaotic launch into adulthood. . . . Or you sit with your wife and wonder what you could have done to make your marriage more loving, intimate and unified.
>
> We don't need to read mystery novels; our own lives are mysteries to us. . . . None of us can say that we go where

we are by careful planning and disciplined administration of the plan. The details tend to confound us all, and we wish we could be let in on the secret. . . .

We all tend to think that if we'd only known the last chapter first, we would have dealt a lot better with what was on our plate. . . . [But] God *has* let us in on the secret. In the Bible, we *are* given the last chapter. The end of it all is laid out for us, God invites each of us to eavesdrop on eternity and then to look back on our lives with the unique perspective that only eternity can give us. God's story only makes sense from the vantage point of eternity, and your life will only make sense when you view it from that perspective.[1]

The older we grow, the stronger death's reality looms. In our culture, death has gradually moved away from our presence. We rarely die in our own space, expiring instead in facilities or institutions; more than 80 percent of deaths are not at home. Many people struggle to know how to respond to the death of a loved one or even how to behave as a family member.

Maybe you'll soon face or already have experienced the death of someone close, and you'll begin to think more about your own coming day. One major midlife task is accepting that you won't always be around and that it's possible you'll die sooner than you think or wish! Such thoughts do bring a feeling of helplessness, because death is something we cannot control.

Mortality is an issue most of us want to avoid. Even we, as believers, who say we have no fear of death, would still like to avoid the whole process. People deny, flee, ignore, and repress death.

Ernest Becker, in *The Denial of Death,* said, "The idea of death, the fear of it, haunts the human animal like nothing else; it is a mainspring of human activity—activity designed largely to void the fatality of death, to overcome it by denying in some way that it is the final destiny for man."[2]

Shakespeare's King Lear said, "The fear of death is worse than death itself."

Billy Graham said, "Christians are not immune to the fear of death. Death is not always a 'beautiful release,' but an enemy which separates. There is a certain mystery to it. It does not respect the young or the old, the good or the evil, the Christian or the heathen."[3]

The Scriptures have much to say too.

His loved ones are very precious to him, and he does not lightly let them die.[4]

It is destined that men die only once, and after that comes judgment.[5]

He will wipe away all tears from their eyes, and there shall be no more death, nor sorrow, nor crying, nor pain. All of that has gone forever.[6]

The End of Transitions

Physical death, basically, is the permanent, irreversible cessation of vital bodily functions. However, not all functions stop at the same time. It used to be that lack of a heartbeat was considered final evidence, but attention has shifted to the brain for a reliable indication of when death has occurred.

Joe Bayly, who, after he and his wife lost three children, wrote *The View From a Hearse,* said that death is a wound to the living.[7]

Why do we shrink from even discussing death? We criticize the Victorians because of their attitude about sex, but, unlike us, they dealt openly with this life's end. *Why* do we fear it so much? There are several reasons.

We fear pain and suffering. We fear the unknown. We fear leaving loved ones and friends. And we fear being alone, even though, again, on average, four of five are dying away from home or familiar surroundings.

Joyce Landorf Heatherley said, in *Mourning Song*:

> Here, then, is part of the answer as to why death frightens us so much. While, as a Christian, I know Christ has removed the sting of death and death can never kill me for eternity—death still exists. It is still fearfully ugly and repulsive. I probably will never be able to regard, imagine or fantasize death as being a loving friend.
>
> Whenever and wherever death and dying connects with us—no matter how strong we are prepared for it—it still slides and slithers into our lives and freezes us with fear. Such is the nature of death.[8]

Cyrus Sulzberger, in *My Brother Death*, said, "Men fear death because they refuse to understand it."[9] In order to understand death, we must deal with our fears of death. But regarding the unknown, we really don't know what it's like to die even when people tell us of "near-death experiences."

We fear being separated from familiar people, places, and things. We fear embarking on a journey from which there's no hope of a return visit. We know we cannot write, phone, or come back.

We're fearful because the tune of death is uncertain even when we're stricken with a terminal illness. Another person is apparently healthy one day and gone the next. We fear that death will be violent, repulsive, disfiguring.

Life is terminal. From birth we're engaged in the process of dying. In middle age some people begin to realize that time is short; others feel that time will soon be up. This awareness can help us evaluate what's truly important and guide us to decide what we'll do with the rest of our time.

In truth, for the believer, death is a transition, a tunnel leading from this world into the next. Perhaps the trip is a bit frightening because we're leaving what security we feel here and going to what's as yet unseen, but without question the final destination will be well worth the present uncertainty.

In *The Secret of Staying in Love*, John Powell presented a beautiful description of this life's finality:

> This book is gratefully dedicated to Bernice. She has been a source of support in many of my previous attempts to write. She has generously contributed an excellent critical eye, a cultivated literary sense and especially a confident kind of encouragement. She did not help with the preparation of this book. On July 11 she received a better offer. She was called by the Creator and the Lord of the Universe to join the celebration at the banquet table of eternal life.[10]

You and I have no choice about the timing of death. And we will die. But we can decide how we view death. We can choose how we'll spend our remaining years.

We also can opt for what to do with our body upon death, determine what we'd like our funeral to reflect, resolve how we want others to remember us, and elect where we'd like to die if that's up to us. We can learn to talk more openly about death, to fear it less, to anticipate how we would handle terminal illness. We can make a choice as to whether or not we'd allow ourselves to be kept alive on life support. We can draw up a will and work out our pros and cons for carrying life insurance.

Most people plan their own weddings. Who will plan your memorial service? Why not plan it or give instructions for it? Since it's for the survivors, why not take the burden of choice off of them and handle the details? Many write an advance obituary to assist the family in pulling together significant details. Think about writing your story, which gives you the opportunity to reflect on your life. For many it's a step of completion as a gift to current family and the next generations. (For additional information on this subject, I encourage you to read *Living Fully in the Shadow of Death*, by Susan Zonnebelt-Smeenge and Robert C. DeVries.[11])

> Biblical precedents have been set for us by some of the great Old Testament believers who gave personal burial instructions. Jacob said, "I am about to be gathered to my people. Bury me with my fathers in the cave in the field of Ephron the Hittite. . . ." After he expressed his wishes, the Bible says, he went peacefully. "When Jacob had finished giving instructions to his sons, he drew his feet up into the bed, breathed his last and was gathered to his people" (Genesis 49:29, 33).
>
> "By faith," the writer tells us, "Joseph, when his end was near . . . gave instructions about his bones" (Hebrews 11:22).
>
> These two great patriarchs didn't use long-range planning, but they had definite arrangements which were made known to their family.[12]

Our faith does not spare us from physical death or from the loss and pain of the grief process. It does offer us hope of completion in Christ's presence.

At the end of a retreat, Archibald Hart shared a story about a pastor's message, which was titled "I pray that you will die before you are finished."

> He was not giving a prayer for an early demise; it was a prayer for a very long and fruitful life. It was a reminder that God's plan is never finished, His work is never done. . . .
>
> Of course, there was a reason why [the "faith heroes" of Hebrews 11] died before they were finished. God is not a killjoy or a sadist who would rob us of final victory just for the fun of it. "God wanted them to wait and share the even better rewards that were prepared for us" (Hebrews 11:40 TLB).

What makes us think we will finish all we want to do before we die? A neurotic need to prove something to ourselves? Some memory of rejection by a parent who said "You'll never amount to anything"? Some uncomfortable inner drive to prove that we're perfect? A hope that people will respect us more if we are successful and powerful? I suspect that the more we want to finish before we die, the more likely we'll die before we're finished. Life is, unfortunately, a chain of incompletes.

A successful life will always be unfinished, and the more successful it is, the more will be left undone. . . . The positive side to all of this is that God is with us in our incompleteness and gives us permission to stop trying to accomplish everything in one brief period of existence. It is liberating to realize that we don't have to finish. All we have to be is faithful.[13]

When you take out a life insurance policy, your agent talks about death benefits. Even without that policy, as a believer you have death benefits too. You'll experience these firsthand; your family will benefit from them as well (the benefits can give them comfort). Consider what they are.

When you die, you'll immediately be with the Lord. You'll be absent from the body and present with Jesus. In God's timing you'll receive your glorified body at Christ's second coming. You will have freedom from evil, and you will be like Jesus in knowledge and in love. Guaranteed!

Dear friends, now we are children of God, and what we will be has not yet been made known. But we know that when Christ appears, we shall be like him, for we shall see him as he is.[14]

At this point or in the near future, you may experience the death of a parent, a close friend, or your spouse. You may soon face the prospect of your own death; many know in advance that they're dying. You cannot run from death, that of another or your own.

Ponder in advance what you will or might experience when you know you're dying. This will help you be better able to handle your inner turmoil and reactions. If someone close to you is dying, knowing what he or she will experience will make you more able to minister.

Preparing Practically

Dying means change. Even when we think we're prepared, we still live with the fear that we won't be able to cope. We're afraid of the kinds of changes that will occur in us and how these changes will affect others.

Perhaps you've heard the phrase "he died well" or used it yourself. What does that expression mean to you? Among other things, maybe it means making peace in your relationships, with God and with others.

Paul Tournier said:

> Death will come for me just as I am, and what happens to me will depend exclusively, as it will for all other men, my brethren, on God's mercy, and not on my preparation, however sincere it may be.
>
> In my view it is the whole of life which is a preparation for death, and I do not see how I can prepare myself any differently today than at any other time. Death is not a project, and it is not my reality. What concerns me is my life now, and to seek the will of God for me today, for the meaning of life seems to me to be always the same, from one end to the other—to allow oneself to be led by God. Detach myself from the world? That would be to run away from my own reality. To empty this time that God still gives me in this world in order to fill it with meditation on death, would, for me, be to give up the belief that my life as it is today has a meaning.[15]

How have you prepared for dying? I know it's not a favorite subject to think about, plan for, or discuss, yet it's on our horizon. Have you clarified the treatment plans if you're hospitalized or institutionalized with a terminal or irreversible illness? Who do you want assisting you, making health care and financial decisions? What burial or interment guidelines do you have in place?

Do you want to participate in or conduct your service? My closest friend and I have determined that each of us will assist in the other's service, but one of us won't be around for that, so we're planning to film what we'll say in advance. What music do you want played? I've already selected one song and hope the CD still exists when I depart. Have you considered making a DVD to play at the service? Think about these issues in depth.

> We avoid death or even fear it because death is an evil, the horrible rending of a person from her body, from loved ones, from the ability to be fully in God's image.
>
> Yet death is also a mercy, it is the final affliction of life's miseries. It is the entrance to life with God. Life's passing can be a beautiful gift of God. This riddle of death's evil and its blessing is not difficult to solve. We enact it every Good Friday as we recall the evil of Christ's death to be followed on Easter Sunday with the joy of his resurrection.
>
> St. Isaac the Syrian instructed:
>
> Prepare your heart for your departure. If you are wise, you will expect it every hour. . . . And when the time of departure comes, go joyfully to meet it, saying, "Come in peace. I knew you would come, and I have not neglected anything that could help me on the journey."[16]

The traditional Christian "art of dying" (*ars moriendi*) is not a denial of the awfulness of death. In fact, we recognize that death is the last enemy[17] and provide the tools that can help to guide believers through their last hours. The Christian's death is an embodiment of faith in a God who has defeated death itself and will give life to our own mortal bodies.[18]

Our dying is a home-going! David Morley described it wonderfully:

> What a joyous moment that will be, when he will be reunited with all of his loved ones who have gone on before! When, once more, the lines of communication will be reestablished, the old voices heard again, and the deathly silence at last broken forever, no more goodbyes, no more quick slipping away of loved ones into the mysterious enigma of death.
>
> The most glorious anticipation of the Christian is that, at the time of death, he will come face-to-face with his blessed Lord, his wonderful, patient Redeemer, who all of those years continued to love him in spite of the countless times the man ignored Him and went his willful way. We will not be encountering a stranger, but the best and the most intimate friend that we have ever had. When we think of death as a time of revelation and reunion, we immediately remove its venom. We can say, with the apostle Paul, "O death, where is thy sting? O grave, where is thy victory?" (1 Corinthians 15:55 KJV).[19]

Questions to Consider:

1. What was your comfort level in reading this chapter?

2. What questions do you have now, afterward?

3. If you were to talk to someone about death or dying, who would it be?

4. What awaits you when you die? Do you have assurance?

God so loved the world that he gave his one and only Son, that whoever believes in him shall not perish but have eternal life.[20]

For Discussion

Chapter 1—Transitions: Friend or Foe?

1. What have been the main transitions and issues you've faced in each of the phases or stages in life's second half?

2. In which cases did you respond in a constructive way? What were those constructive ways?

3. What are some of the endings you've experienced over the past ten years, and how have you responded to them?

4. Describe your most recent transitions and how they've impacted you.

Chapter 2—We, the Boomers

1. Describe your reactions to being called a "baby boomer."

2. Which characteristics described you, and which didn't?

3. Consider and discuss the questions summarized from Kay Strom's book (*The Second-Half Adventure*) near the end of the chapter.

Chapter 3—The Never-Ending Seasons of Parenting

1. Describe what changed during your first year of parenting.

2. Which parenting stage(s) are you in now, and how are you handling it?

3. What are the losses and gains of your parenting stage at this time?

4. Discuss your answers and responses on the lists at chapter's end.

Chapter 4—Midlife Matters

1. "To me, midlife means _____."

2. "My greatest adjustment in midlife has been, is, or will be _____."

3. If you're married, in what way(s) is your spouse "the right one"?

4. If you're unmarried, in what way would a person be "right" for you?

5. What advice would you share with others on how to prepare for the second half of marriage?

Chapter 5—"The Empty Nest," or "The Emergence"?

1. If you're in this stage, describe your responses to it during the first three months. Describe also your spouse's responses.

2. How did the empty nest impact your marriage?

3. What's been the most difficult part of detaching from your children?

4. Discuss your responses to this chapter's questions on career, retirement, etc. (in the section **Progressing Proactively**).

Chapter 6—The Second Half of Marriage

1. Take some time and think about your wedding vows. What were they? Perhaps you can find them and discuss them.

2. If you were to create vows for the second half of your marriage, what would they be?

3. Discuss and describe your responses to the questions and suggestions for evaluating your marriage.

4. What are four of your goals for the remainder of your marriage?

Chapter 7—The Boomerang Generation

1. If your child has ever returned home, describe how it impacted you and your marriage.

2. If your child were to return, what would you do to adjust?

3. What do you appreciate about your adult children, and what have you learned from them?

Chapter 8—The Gathering of Losses

1. Describe the losses you've experienced during the past ten years.

2. What were your responses to the four questions about parents' death?

3. Which losses described in this chapter did you identify with most?

4. What has helped you the most in handling your losses?

Chapter 9—You're Older: Rejoice!

1. Describe the pluses and the minuses of your age at this time of life.

2. Discuss your responses to Patrick Morley's "audit item" suggestions.

3. What are you letting go of during your current stage?

Chapter 10—A Reflective Life

1. Describe a special moment you've had with a family member.

2. If you had a hundred days left for yourself, how would you use them?

3. What would you say is sacred in your life?

4. What could you do now in your life to ensure that you've loved well?

Chapter 11—Alone Again

1. When you experienced grief over the loss of a loved one, which "crazy" emotions did you feel?

2. What Scriptures have been of help to you during times of grief?

3. If you've lost a spouse, what was your greatest adjustment? If you haven't, what do you think would be your greatest adjustment?

Chapter 12—Married Again?

1. What would you say are the major adjustments for those who remarry?

2. What do you think are three crucial questions a remarrying couple must ask?

3. What do you believe about prenuptial agreements?

4. What are issues and benefits you've seen in your friends' remarriages?

Chapter 13—Retire, or Redirect and Restructure?

1. What's your response to the word *retirement*?

2. If you've already retired, what's been your biggest adjustment? If you haven't, what do you think will be your adjustments?

3. Describe what you want to do with the rest of your life.

4. Talk about your reactions and answers to the questions about handling your next phase (in the section **Our True Foundation and Calling**).

Chapter 14—Your Purpose Now

1. What do you believe is your purpose in life at this time?

2. Discuss how you answered the Rick Warren questions (in the section **Purpose With Passion**).

3. Describe the passion you have in your life right now.

Chapter 15—The Legacy You'll Leave

1. What legacy did your parents leave for you?

2. What do you believe is part of the legacy you will leave to others?

3. Describe what goes into your ethical will.

Chapter 16—The Last Chapter

1. What does death mean to you?

2. If someone asked how long you think you'll live and how you might die, what would you say? (Yes, it's a difficult question.)

3. What do you want your funeral or memorial service to reflect?

4. Talk about your answers to the last four questions in this chapter.

Notes

Introduction

1. Joshua 14:6–14, emphasis added.

Chapter 1: Transitions: Friend or Foe?

1. Charles M. Sell, *Transition: The Stages of Adult Life* (Chicago: Moody, 1985), xi.

2. Printed with permission from Many Rivers Press, www.davidwhyte .com. David Whyte, "What to Remember When Waking" in *The House of Belonging* (Langley, Washington: Many Rivers Press).

3. William Bridges, *The Way of Transition: Embracing Life's Most Difficult Moments* (Cambridge, MA: Perseus, 2001), 5–6.

4. William Bridges, *Managing Transitions: Making the Most of Change* (Cambridge, MA: DaCapo, 2004), adapted, 15–16.

5. See Bridges, *The Way of Transition*, 21.

6. Ibid., 3.

7. Adapted from the Holmes-Rahe Stress Scale. See Thomas H. Holmes and Richard H. Rahe, "Stress Rating Scale" in *Journal of Psychiatric Research* (1967: II), 216.

8. Ann Kaiser Stearns, *Living Through Personal Crisis* (New York: Ballantine, 1984, 2010), 65–66.

9. See Bridges, *Managing Transitions,* 22–23.

10. See David C. Morley, *Halfway Up the Mountain* (Old Tappan, NJ: Revell, 1979), 26.

11. See 2 Corinthians 12:9.

12. Adapted from concept in Lorry Lutz, *Looking Forward to the Rest of Your Life? Embracing Midlife and Beyond* (Grand Rapids: Baker, 2004), 24.

13. See Bridges, *Managing Transitions,* 87.

14. Morley, *Halfway Up the Mountain,* 85–86.

Chapter 2: We, the Boomers

1. C. S. Lewis, *The Allegory of Love* (London: Oxford University Press, 1938), n.p.

2. See Gary R. Collins and Timothy E. Clinton, *Baby Boomer Blues* (Waco, TX: Word, 1992), 42–49.

3. See Hans Finzel, *Help! I'm a Baby Boomer* (Wheaton, IL: Victor, 1989), 14–15.

4. See Collins and Clinton, *Baby Boomer Blues,* 81.

5. See Morris Massey, *The People Puzzle* (Reston, VA: Reston, 1979), 80–99.

6. See ibid., 99.

7. Kay Marshall Strom, *The Second-Half Adventure: Don't Just Retire—Use Your Time, Skills and Resources to Change the World* (Chicago: Moody, 2009), 29.

8. Proverbs 15:22

9. Strom, *Second-Half Adventure,* adapted, 60–65.

Chapter 3: The Never-Ending Seasons of Parenting

1. Barbara C. Unell and Jerry L. Wyckoff, *The Eight Seasons of Parenthood: How the Stages of Parenting Constantly Reshape Our Adult Identities* (New York: Crown, 2000), 4.

2. These "seasons" are extensively described and explained in Unell and Wyckoff, ibid.

3. Ibid., 27.

4. Ibid., adapted, 29–30.

5. R. Scott Sullender, *Losses in Later Life* (New York: Paulist, 1989), 61.

Chapter 4: Midlife Matters

1. Paul Tripp, *Lost in the Middle: Midlife and the Grace of God* (Wapualopen, PA: Shepherd, 2004), 39.

2. See more extensive treatment in ibid., 38–41.

3. Dr. Dan B. Allender, *The Wounded Heart* (Colorado Springs: Nav-Press, 1995), 30.

4. Alyce Faye Cleese and Brian Bates, *How to Manage Your Mother: Understanding the Most Difficult, Complicated, and Fascinating Relationship in Your Life* (New York: HarperCollins, 2000), 8–9.

5. See Psalm 139.

6. Dwight Hervey Small, *When Christians Retire: Finding New Purpose in Your Bonus Years* (Kansas City: Beacon Hill, 2000), 62.

7. See Robert A. Johnson and Jerry M. Ruhl, Ph.D., *Living Your Unlived Life: Coping with Unrealized Dreams and Fulfilling Your Purpose in the Second Half of Life* (New York: Tarcher, 2009), 3–5.

8. Lloyd H. Ahlem, *Do I Have to Be Me? The Psychology of Human Need* (Ventura, CA: Regal, 1973), n.p.

9. Tripp, *Lost in the Middle*, 280.

10. From "No One," 1970, by Linda Rich. Assigned to InterVarsity Christian Fellowship of the USA.

11. See Tripp, *Lost in the Middle*, 277–286.

12. Romans 12:2 niv1984.

13. Adapted from Harold Ivan Smith, *Life Changing Answers to Depression* (Eugene, OR: Harvest House, 1978), 66–68.

14. Matthew 6:33

Chapter 5: "The Empty Nest," or "The Emergence"?

1. Betty L. Polston, Ph.D., with Susan K. Golant, M.A., *Loving Midlife Marriage: A Guide to Keeping Romance Alive From the Empty Nest Through Retirement* (New York: John Wiley & Sons, 1999), 49–50.

2. On this observation, see ibid.

3. See ibid., 50–57.

4. Gail Sheehy, *New Passages: Mapping Your Life Across Time* (New York: Random, 1996), 319.

5. Robert Lee and Marjorie Casebier, *The Spouse Gap: Weathering the Marriage Crisis During Middlescence* (Nashville: Abingdon, 1971), 132.

6. R. Scott Sullender, *Losses in Later Life* (New York: Paulist, 1989), 68.

7. Paul and Jeannie McKean, *Leading a Child to Independence* (San Bernardino, CA: Here's Life, 1986), 21.

8. Adapted from Polston, with Golant, *Loving Midlife Marriage,* 79–80.

9. Lee and Casebier, *The Spouse Gap*, 132.

10. James A. Peterson, *Married Love in the Middle Years* (Chicago: Association, 1968), 52–53.

11. Polston, with Golant, *Loving Midlife Marriage*, 25.

12. Unell and Wyckoff, *The Eight Seasons of Parenthood*, 229. This is the seventh of their eight "seasons."

13. Polston, with Golant, *Loving Midlife Marriage*, 89–90.

Chapter 6: The Second Half of Marriage

1. David and Claudia Arp, *The Second Half of Marriage: Facing the Eight Challenges of the Empty-Nest Years* (Grand Rapids: Zondervan, 1998), 27.

2. Ecclesiastes 3:1 KJV

3. Daniel J. Levinson, *The Seasons of a Man's Life* (New York: Ballantine, 1978), 6–7.

4. Thornton Wilder, "The Skin of Our Teeth" from *3 Plays* (New York: Perennial, 1998), 200.

5. See Gary Thomas, *Sacred Marriage* (Grand Rapids: Zondervan, 2000), 39.

6. See John F. Cuber and Peggy B. Haroff, "The More Total View: Relationships Between Men and Women of the Upper Middle Class" in *Marriage and Family Living* (1963: 25), adapted, 140–145.

7. David and Vera Mace, *We Can Have Better Marriages If We Really Want Them* (Nashville: Abingdon, 1978), 30.

Chapter 7: The Boomerang Generation

1. H. Norman Wright, *Loving a Prodigal: A Survival Guide for Parents of Rebellious Children* (Colorado Springs: Victor, 1999), 149.

2. See Dorothy Weiss Gottlieb, Inez Bellow Gottlieb, and Marjorie A. Slavin, *What to Do When Your Son or Daughter Divorces* (New York: Bantam, 1988), 37.

3. Jay Kesler, *Grandparenting: The Agony and the Ecstasy* (Ann Arbor: Servant, 1994), 16.

4. Ibid.

Chapter 8: The Gathering of Losses

1. Judith Viorst, *Necessary Losses* (New York: Simon & Schuster, 1986), 269.

2. R. Scott Sullender, *Losses in Later Life* (New York: Paulist, 1989), 43.

3. Carol Staudacher, *Beyond Grief* (Oakland: New Harbinger, 1989), 82.

4. See ibid., 73.

5. Ibid., 94.

6. Fiona Marshall, *Losing a Parent* (Cambridge, MA: Fisher, 2000), 45.

7. Dennis Klass, Phyllis R. Silverman, and Steven L. Nickman, *Continuing Bonds: New Understandings of Grief* (Philadelphia: Taylor and Francis, 1996), 76–81.

8. See Therese A. Rando, *Grieving: How To Go On Living When Someone You Love Dies* (Lexington, MA: Lexington, 1988), 135–151.

9. See Marshall, *Losing a Parent*, 19–21.

10. Sullender, *Losses in Later Life,* 43.

11. See ibid., 88.

12. Ibid., 51.

Chapter 9: You're Older: Rejoice!

1. James Hillman, *The Force of Character and the Lasting Life* (New York: Random, 1999), 18.

2. See Lutz, *Looking Forward to the Rest of Your Life? Embracing Midlife and Beyond*, 73–78.

3. See Leviticus 19:32.

4. See Job 12:20; 15:10; 32:7.

5. See Exodus 20:12.

6. See Genesis 27:1; 48:10; 1 Samuel 3:2; 1 Kings 14:4; 2 Samuel 19:35; 1 Kings 1:1–4.

7. Ecclesiastes 12:1–5

8. See, for example, the blessing of Abraham in Genesis 15:15.

9. Psalm 71:9, 18

10. Psalm 37:25

11. See Tim Stafford, *As Our Years Increase: Loving, Caring, Preparing* (New York: HarperCollins, 1991), 28–29.

12. Patrick Morley, *Second Wind for the Second Half* (Grand Rapids: Zondervan, 1999), 18.

13. Todd T. W. Daly, "Chasing Methuselah" in *Christianity Today* (Jan. 2011): adapted, 18–20.

14. See Rob Moll, *The Art of Dying: Living Fully Into the Life to Come* (Downers Grove, IL: IVP, 2010), 147.

15. Morley, *Second Wind for the Second Half*, 167.

16. See Andrew Weil, M.D., *Healthy Aging: A Lifelong Guide to Your Well-Being* (Harpswell, ME: Anchor, 2007), 107–108.

17. Unell and Wyckoff, *The Eight Seasons of Parenthood,* 16. (This is the eighth of their eight "seasons.")

18. William Sadler, Ph.D. *The Third Age: Six Principles for Personal Growth and Rejuvenation After Forty* (Cambridge, MA: DaCapo, 2000), 164.

19. Adapted from ibid., 160–164.

20. See Sheehy, *New Passages: Mapping Your Life Across Time,* 426.

21. Ibid., 424–425.

22. See Norman Doidge, M.D., *The Brain That Changes Itself* (New York: Penguin, 2007), xiv; 84–90.

23. Zaldy S. Tan, M.D., MPH, *Age-Proof Your Mind* (New York: Warner, 2006), 6.

24. Adapted from Paula Payne Hardin, *What Are You Doing With the Rest of Your Life?* (San Rafael, CA: New World Library, 1992), 29–30.

25. Ibid., 214.

26. Dr. Paul Tournier, *Learn to Grow Old* (London: SCM, 1971), 174–175.

27. Ibid., 178.

28. Ibid., 185.

29. Jeremiah 29:11

30. Jeremiah 33:3

31. As quoted in Tournier, *Learn to Grow Old,* 192.

32. Tournier, *Learn to Grow Old,* 210–211.

Chapter 10: A Reflective Life

1. Ken Gire, *The Reflective Life: Becoming More Spiritually Sensitive to the Everyday Moments of Life* (Colorado Springs: Chariot Victor, 1998), 36.

2. Ibid., 37–38.

3. See Don Aslett, *How to Have a 48-Hour Day* (Cincinnati: Better, 1996), 39.

4. See Tim Hansel, *When I Relax I Feel Guilty* (Elgin, IL: David C. Cook, 1979), 69.

5. See Leslie B. Flynn, *It's About Time* (Newtown, PA, Timothy, 1974), 24.

6. H. Norman Wright, *Finding the Life You've Been Looking for: The Surprising Power of Simple Living* (Eugene, OR: Harvest House, 2006), 38–40.

7. 1 Chronicles 28:9 AMP

8. Psalm 1:2 NLT

9. J. I. Packer, *Knowing God* (Downers Grove, IL: InverVarsity Press, 1973), 18–19.

10. Matthew 22:37, 39–40; see also Romans 13:8–10.

11. Gire, *The Reflective Life,* 85–86.

Chapter 11: Alone Again

1. Joanne T. Jozefowski, *The Phoenix Phenomenon: Rising From the Ashes of Grief* (Northvale, NJ: Jason Aronson, 1999), 17.

2. H. Norman Wright, *Experiencing Grief* (Nashville: B&H, 2004).

3. H. Norman Wright, *Reflections of a Grieving Spouse: The Unexpected Journey From Loss to Renewed Hope* (Eugene, OR: Harvest House, 2009).

4. Staudacher, *Beyond Grief,* 56–60.

5. See Wright, *Reflections of a Grieving Spouse,* 18.

6. See ibid., 5.

Chapter 12: Married Again?

1. Ron L. Deal and David H. Olson, *The Remarriage Checkup: Tools to Help Your Marriage Last a Lifetime* (Minneapolis: Bethany House, 2010), 40.

2. See H. Norman Wright, *Before You Remarry* (Eugene, OR: Harvest House, 1988), 14–15.

3. See Neal A. Kuyper, "The Question of Children at the Wedding" in Belovitc, 122–123.

4. See Jim Smoke, *Growing in Remarriage* (Old Tappan, NJ: Revell, 1990), 90.

Chapter 13: Retire, or Redirect and Restructure?

1. *The Concise Oxford Dictionary* (New York: Oxford University Press).

2. Howard G. Hendricks, "Rethinking Retirement" in *Bibliotheca Sacra* (April 2000: 157), 626.

3. Dwight Harvey Small, *When Christians Retire: Finding New Purpose in Your Bonus Years* (Kansas City: Beacon Hill, 2000), 15.

4. Viorst, *Necessary Losses,* 237.

5. Ibid., 325–326.

6. Small, *When Christians Retire,* 13.

7. *Merriam-Webster's Collegiate Dictionary*, Eleventh Edition (Springfield, MA: Merriam-Webster Inc., 2008), 792.

8. Small, *When Christians Retire*, 58.

9. Peter Kreeft, *Heaven: The Heart's Deepest Longing* (San Francisco: Ignatius, 1989), 75.

10. Jules Z. Willing, *The Reality of Retirement* (New York: William Morrow and Co., 1981), 30.

11. See Richard Exley, *The Rhythm of Life* (Tulsa: Honor, 1987), adapted, 22–23.

12. See also Small, *When Christians Retire*, 106–108.

13. 2 Timothy 4:6–8 *Phillips*

Chapter 14: Your Purpose Now

1. *About Schmidt*. Directed by Alexander Payne; based on the novel by Louis Begley. New Line Cinema: 2002.

2. See Richard J. Leiter and David A. Shapiro, *Something to Live For: Finding Your Way in the Second Half of Life* (San Francisco: Berrett-Koehler, 2008), 21.

3. Ibid.,169–170.

4. Jim Stovall, *The Ultimate Gift* (Colorado Springs: David C. Cook, 2001).

5. *Saving Private Ryan*. Directed by Steven Spielberg. DreamWorks SKG: 1998.

6. Rick Warren, *The Purpose Driven Life* (Grand Rapids: Zondervan, 2007), 30.

7. Isaiah 26:3 GNT

8. Warren, *The Purpose Driven Life*, 30–34.

9. Johnson and Ruhl, *Living Your Unlived Life,* 1.

10. Ibid., 4.

11. Psalm 34:18

12. Psalm 145:14

13. Isaiah 49:4

14. Job 7:6, 19 TLB

15. Ephesians 1:11–12 THE MESSAGE

16. Warren, *The Purpose Driven Life,* 92–93.

17. Dr. Paul Brand and Philip Yancey, *In His Image* (Grand Rapids: Zondervan, 1984), 46.

18. Ibid., 47.

19. 2 Timothy 1:9 TLB

20. 1 Peter 2:9 GWT

21. Ephesians 5:17 TLB

22. Romans 12:3 PHILLIPS

23. 2 Corinthians 5:18 TLB

24. Philippians 3:10–11 NIV1984

Chapter 15: The Legacy You'll Leave

1. Tim Kimmel, *Legacy of Love: A Plan for Parenting on Purpose* (Portland, OR: Multnomah, 1989), n.p.

2. Ibid.

3. 1 Peter 4:10 AMP

4. Andrew Weil, *Healthy Aging* (New York: Knopf, 2003), n.p., as quoted in Leiter and Shapiro, *Something to Live For*, 68.

5. See Susan Zonnebelt-Smeenge and Robert C. DeVries, *Living Fully in the Shadow of Death: Assurance and Guidance to Finish Well* (Grand Rapids: Baker, 2004), adapted, 111–112.

6. Adapted from Linda Ellis and Mac Anderson, *The Dash: Making a Difference with Your Life* (Naperville, IL: Simple Truths, 2006).

Chapter 16: The Last Chapter

1. Tripp, *Lost in the Middle*, 294–295, italics mine.

2. Ernest Becker, *The Denial of Death* (New York: Free Press, 1973), 15.

3. Billy Graham, *Facing Death and the Life After* (Waco, TX: Word, 1987), 25.

4. Psalm 116:15 TLB

5. Hebrews 9:27 TLB

6. Revelation 21:4 TLB

7. Joseph T. Bayly, *The View From a Hearse* (Colorado Springs: David C. Cook, 1973).

8. Joyce Landorf Heatherley, *Mourning Song* (Old Tappan, NJ: Revell, 1974), 26.

9. Cyrus Leo Sulzberger, *My Brother Death* (New York: Harper & Brothers, 1961).

10. John Powell, *The Secret of Staying in Love* (Niles, IL: Argus, 1974).

11. Susan Zonnebelt-Smeenge and Robert C. DeVries, *Living Fully in the Shadow of Death: Assurance and Guidance to Finish Well* (Grand Rapids: Baker, 2004).

12. Graham, *Facing Death and the Life After*, 201–202.

13. Archibald Hart, original source unknown.

14. 1 John 3:2

15. Tournier, *Learn to Grow Old*, 190.

16. Moll, *The Art of Dying*, 26.

17. See 1 Corinthians 15:26.

18. See Moll, *The Art of Dying*, 26, 68.

19. Morley, *Halfway Up the Mountain*, 77–78.

20. John 3:16

H. NORMAN WRIGHT is a licensed marriage, family, and child therapist, as well as a certified trauma specialist. The author of more than seventy books, Norman Wright has pioneered premarital counseling programs throughout the country and conducts seminars on many subjects, including marriage enrichment, parenting, and grief recovery. His current focus is on crisis and trauma counseling and critical incident debriefings within the wider community. He lives in Bakersfield, California.